STAND strong

ELLEN HARBIN

Scriptures marked NIV are taken from the NEW INTERNATIONAL
VERSION (NIV): Scripture taken from THE HOLY BIBLE, NEW
INTERNATIONAL VERSION ®. Copyright© 1973, 1978, 1984, 2011 by
Biblica, Inc.™. Used by permission of Zondervan

Scriptures marked KJV are taken from the KING JAMES VERSION (KJV):
KING JAMES VERSION, public domain.

ISBN: 9781726036672

SLOW Livin' Publishing
Fraser, MI

ellenharbin.com

DEDICATION

To Kevin

Your passionate pursuit of Jesus and devotion as His disciple,
your covenant love and commitment to me,
your unshakable love and wise counsel to our children,
and your faithful leadership as a pastor
evidences you stand strong.

CONTENTS

ACKNOWLEDGMENTS

I am forever grateful to those who share their talent, expertise, and wisdom. Your involvement and support is appreciated.

Jenny Johnson – cover design
Joe Cummings – author photo
Jerry Cummings – cover photo
The Sequel – writing warriors
Melena Cummings – business advisor
Erin and Jeanne – wisdom & guidance
ACCESS prayer team – Christ Church Fraser

Kevin – doing life with you is never dull. Your devotion and commitment to our oneness encourages me every day. Thank you, for loving me well and cheering me on. I am, and always will be, devoted to you.

INTRODUCTION

Welcome to the second book in the STAND series. For years I have written and taught Bible Studies, and though groups have varied over the years, one question is consistently asked. "When will your studies be published?" The STAND series is the answer to their appeal.

When we attempt to follow Jesus on our own strength, we stumble and fall on our faith journey. Isaiah 7:9b speaks to this futile effort. "If you do not stand firm in your faith, you will not stand at all." Weary, weak, and worn-out followers are not able to stand strong if we're not continually face to face with Jesus. We're strengthened and steadied when we stand firm.

It's my prayer you'll be encouraged to grow, challenged to change, and influenced to live as Jesus intends as you meet a few individuals from the Book of Mark. And like them, when we're weary, weak, and worn out we're desperate for a face-to-face encounter with Jesus.

Throughout each chapter **KEY POINTS** are intentionally emphasized to encourage you to stand strong. At the end of each chapter four recurring sections provide opportunity for in-depth personal study or to assist in facilitating group discussions.

PONDER: to deeply, carefully, and thoughtfully consider

PERSUADE: God's Word influences, encourages, and guides

PRACTICAL: applying Biblical Truth to present day

PERSONAL: inviting Jesus into your current reality

Jesus, come and open the eyes of our hearts.
Holy Spirit, be our Teacher and shine Your light,
exposing the places in us that
need Your strength.
And, Lord, pour Your wisdom and counsel
into the holes of our hearts
so we can wholeheartedly
stand strong.
In Jesus' name, amen.

When your words came, I ate them;
they were my joy and my heart's delight,
for I bear your name,
O Lord God Almighty.

Jeremiah 15:16

Ellen Harbin

1
strength for the BUSY

"She dresses herself with strength..."
Proverbs 31:17

Prominently displayed on the refrigerator in my kitchen is our family calendar. No one writes on it without first consulting me. I've declared myself the boss of the massive, papered rectangle front and center on the tall appliance. *Look; don't touch* is the unspoken rule understood by every Harbin.

Are you familiar with the quote, "If the Devil can't make you bad, he'll make you busy?" What about the popular expression from the late 1900's, "The Devil made me do it"? Though I believe distraction is one of Satan's mode of operations, I can't blame him for the entries filling my family's calendar or the bullet points on my to-do lists. He's never grabbed a mechanical pencil (because pen is not allowed) and inserted his agenda on the massive papered calendar. My handwriting consumes the lines within the daily squares keeping our individual schedules organized.

To be clear, the Devil can't make you bad – he can entice you to sin, but he can't *make* you do anything. In the first chapter of book one in the STAND series, *STAND unashamed*, I introduce and describe Satan. Summarizing, he distracts, he deceives, and he destroys. Busy is just another one of his tactics, a scheme or strategy, to get us distracted and deceived to believe busy is an acceptable life-style while destroying peace and order.

My husband, Kevin, is a pastor; therefore, Sunday is a

work day. One of God's commands is to observe the Sabbath, a day of rest. Those who commonly work 9-5, Monday through Friday, take Sunday as their Sabbath. Monday is ours, and we take them seriously, because we need serious rest. Are we a busy family? If our calendar were the only source for an answer, you'd exclaim, "Absolutely!" But busy isn't why we rest.

Not long ago, Kevin and I were enjoying a Monday, sipping mugs of coffee and discussing calendars when my husband said, "We need to consider this concept of *busy*." He went on to explain how busy has become a state of being and gets expressed as an emotion when it's the unfitting response to the familiar question, *how are you*. His goal was to get us thinking differently and converse about how we misuse the word *busy*.

I'm guilty. More times than I care to admit, I've responded with the nonsensical response of *busy* when asked the common question, "How are you?" My response reveals *what* I am rather than *how* I'm doing. When did busy become a state of being? Why have I acted like it's acceptable?

When Kevin shined a light on busy, its grip on me was revealed. Busy was holding on because I had allowed it. Busy became my state of being and defined me – almost characterizing my identity. When busy became my go-to answer to the common question, I believed it was an accurate depiction. Being busy somehow translated to being useful.

I was deceived to believe the more I did, the more Jesus was served and glorified. After all, doesn't busy equal fruitful? That's what Satan would have us believe. Busy brought chaos and confusion and made me weary, weak, and worn-out. How is that useful or fruitful?

God doesn't dwell in, or contribute to, chaos and

confusion. He is a God of order, and His Son is the best example of how to live a full life rather than a busy one. You see, Jesus wasn't busy, He was faithful and obedient to God's work. His days were filled with assignments, appointments, and agendas. Kevin and I don't want to live busy, but we do like being active. Busy brings chaos and confusion, active results in accomplishing success toward kingdom growth.

KEY POINT: JESUS DIDN'T COME TO EARTH TO BE BUSY

In Mark 1:21-34 we see Jesus teaching in the synagogue, driving out an evil spirit, and healing a woman from a fever. News about Him spread quickly, and within hours He was performing many more miracles. And all of it, on the same day. Jesus didn't depend on a to-do list. He didn't have a color-coded calendar reminding Him of His next face-to-face encounter.

When Jesus left heaven and put on flesh, His steps were ordered by God. Jesus didn't come to earth to be busy. He came to do His Father's will. John ends his gospel, "Jesus did many other things as well. If every one of them were written down, I suppose that even the whole world would not have room for the books that would be written."

Doesn't that imply Jesus was busy? Sure. Busy isn't bad – how it's managed is what matters. With Jesus, busy is simultaneously active and attentive, fully mastered in His capable hands. Not me...I struggle giving both activity and attentiveness my undivided attention. Active turns to busy, and I'm no longer able to be attentive with weak, weary, and worn-out looming.

The first chapter of Mark introduces us to a woman. Based on the story, we can assume she knew busy. Let's picture ourselves in this narrative. Mark 1:29 says *they* left one place, and *they* went to another. We are a part of *they*. We've left the synagogue and arrive at the home of Simon and Andrew. And it's a good thing because we're all hungry and tired. Some in our group have experienced life-changing transitions on this very day. They've left their jobs and their homes and their families. All because Jesus, God-with-skin-on, called to them, and they chose to follow Him.

Following Jesus requires leaving something. In Mark 1:18 it's recorded, "At once they left their nets…" These fishermen couldn't follow Jesus and remain seaside. They had a decision to make: remain holding the net or leave it behind. Jesus bid them come, and they dropped their nets. They left everything to follow Jesus.

KEY POINT: A RADICAL CALL INVITES RADICAL TRUST AND INVOLVES RADICAL RISK

After *they* left their nets, another set of *they* left theirs, and apparently more *theys* have left things/people/jobs because we're all following Jesus to the synagogue. We're amazed at His words. He teaches with an authority we've not seen in others. (Mark 1:22) Radical is right! Here we are, amongst the crowd, in the synagogue. Do you hear that? It sounds like a growl that quickly turned to a howl. The guttural outburst came from a man. Every one of us takes a step back. It's apparent something is terribly wrong with this man.

His outburst combined with his wild appearance disturbs us. He's deranged, a nut case really. Who allowed this uncontrolled, maniacal lunatic in the synagogue? Someone behind us whispers the answer. "He's obviously possessed by an evil spirit." Another agrees and adds,

"Yes, he is unclean – polluted by evil." My cynical skepticism questions, "What is he doing here?" Audible words from the crazy man become my answer.

"What do you want with us, Jesus…have you come to destroy us? I know who you are…" (Mark 1:24) Whoa. Intakes of breath are heard all around. Everyone freezes, wide-eyed, shocked by this audacious confrontation. One moment all eyes are on Jesus with ears turned and tuned to His words, captivated by this man we're curiously yet cautiously following. Others standing nearby have recently (and radically) trusted to follow Jesus. Until the manic cried out, eyes and ears were on Jesus, but now the crazy one's disruption has diverted our gaze. Everyone seems distracted by the louder voice. Everyone, that is, except for the two sets of fishermen.

When Jesus called the brothers away [see Mark 1:19-20] without delay, they left their business, their father, their employees and started following Jesus. He called, "Come, follow me," and they obeyed His voice. They don't know Him, but they're willing to follow Him. That seems crazy all in itself. You and I are just innocent bystanders watching the events of this day unfold. We can tell there's something special about this Jesus. That men would walk away from their known security, leave what's comfortable and follow this Man, is drastic. A radical risk, for sure.

Extreme. Unconventional. Unorthodox. This radical call from Jesus evokes a radical trust. It must! These men have walked away from everything, and yet, they're not focused on what's behind – not one of them has looked back. They're willingly following the one who called. They're not even familiar with His voice, but still they follow. I'm awed by this radical trust, astonished at the risk they're willing to take.

Yes, this outburst has distracted many, but I'm curious

how the former fishermen react. As I scan the crowd, I notice they're riveted by Jesus, eyes firmly on Him. It's like they're each in their own personal face-to-face encounter. They're not distracted or diverted by the louder voice. "Be quiet!" interrupts my curiosity. The stern command is followed with "Come out of him!" [Mark 1:25] The voice of Jesus has my attention. There's something about the way He speaks – have you noticed? His voice is firm, yet gentle; commanding, yet, comforting. He didn't scream, He wasn't out-of-control – in fact, He never wavered, and He didn't misstep. Rather, He rebuked the evil that had taken over this man. I was annoyed by the interruption of this distraction, but Jesus is ready to relieve and help the unclean man. Jesus is always ready to confront evil and free anyone from its mess.

KEY POINT: EVIL spelled backward is LIVE

Can you believe this? Are you seeing what I'm seeing? Jesus commanded evil out of this man. The same voice that called fishermen to a radical life-change is now Commander over evil.

A battle of ownership over this possessed man ensued. Immediately following the stern command from Jesus, the evil spirit messed with the unclean man, throwing him into convulsions. Jesus now has my full and undivided attention. Yes, a man is violently shaking on the ground, but more riveting and captivating is the one who commands evil to leave the one possessed.

Evil holds on tightly, but Jesus is stronger. Evil threw the man to the ground, but Jesus stood His ground. With Jesus calling the shots, the same voice that called men to follow now calls out evil from a man. Evil's only choice is to vacate because it was called out by Jesus. Evil asked,

"Have you come to destroy us?" and Jesus answered with action. He responded with authority. Evil hinders living, choking the life out of the one it possesses. Evil deceives and desires to kill, steal, and destroy. As Jesus speaks, He drives out evil. At His command, Jesus can undo, untangle, send out, unleash, unchain, unshackle, and call out evil.

As evil was expelled from the man, an unintelligible shriek escaped. Jesus has the last word. A man lay exhausted on the ground, but he has new life; he's been restored. Evil is under the authority and command of Jesus. Therefore, when the call to come out came, evil left. And this man can now truly live.

How can we keep this quiet? We must tell others! So much has happened in just a few short hours. People need to hear, they need to know, they need to see for themselves who Jesus is and what He's capable of. How will they know if we keep silent? Look! Jesus is leaving the synagogue and we should follow. In this growing group of *they*, some are called to follow, and some follow out of curiosity. Which are you?

I can tell we're approaching the home of Simon and Andrew. They're well-known fishermen. We are a hungry and tired group of followers, still reeling from the day's events. Some of us are weak, some weary, and I, like others, am worn-out. If we're going to keep following, we need rest and food to give us strength.

Simon's mother-in-law has a solid reputation. She often roams about the market, picking up whatever she needs to cook her next feast. I've been in awe of the revolving door at this house. There are always visitors — she's best known for her hospitality and feeding all who enter. She serves mostly fish, of course, but, oh, her bread! My mouth waters as we near her house. I can't wait for the familiar smell of freshly baked bread. The woman never quits – her busyness doesn't allow her any down time. It makes perfect sense we'd land at Simon and Andrew's house.

Stepping out of the narrative, look at Mark 1:29. They left, and they went. It's the *theys* that make me pay closer attention as this story unfolds. They leave the synagogue, and they arrive at Simon and Andrew's house. And *they* have expectations. They expect to rest. They expect to eat. Some will need to externally process the day's events and others will hope for quiet reflection. Perhaps they have questions for Jesus. Maybe they feel the need for further explanation of all they experienced.

The expectations they had when this day began have been ignored or forgotten. Nothing about this day was in their original plan. Nothing about this day was normal. I imagine a bit of food and some rest would be good for this weary and worn-out group.

As I read Mark 1:30, I think, "Oh, no – these people are in HALT." Though it's unknown who to credit, this brilliant acronym has grown in popularity. *H*ungry. *A*ngry. *L*onely. *T*ired. H.A.L.T. Each is a physical condition inciting heightened emotions. Individually, or even combined with another, each contributes explanation for certain behavior and emotive reactions.

They're met at the door with news that Simon's mother-in-law is down, weakened by a fever. This busy woman is not able to meet their needs. Hungry and tired, plus unmet expectations equal a recipe for disaster.

Does it seem your work is never done? Have you ever been so busy that a cold, a headache, a muscle ache, a sore bone can't knock you down? There's so much to do. You've plowed through it all, ignoring your sore spot, disregarding your aching muscles, popping Tylenol for the pounding head, avoiding the fact that your throat is on fire – whatever the physical issue, you're moving on because, after all, the work must get done.

Christmas Eve, 1999. Much work needed to be done. Cooking, baking, cleaning, wrapping, mothering, church prep; it was all on my lengthy to-do list. On that morning, I felt busier than busy. However, later that day, I was knocked down. Kevin and I had decided to host both of our extended family's holiday festivities. And I missed it all. I was knocked down –

physically, emotionally, and mentally I was weary, weak, and worn-out.

KEY POINT: STRENGTH COMES THROUGH UNMET EXPECTATIONS

I had expectations galore that Christmas. All went unmet. I didn't have time to be knocked down. I expected to cook, bake, clean, and oversee two major Christmas celebrations. I was a busy woman who had certain expectations. But the ruptured and herniated discs in my back had me in serious HALT – replacing hungry with hurting. On Christmas Day, I was admitted to the hospital for a five day stay...absent from all family fun. Physical weakness combined with unmet expectations wreaked havoc, making me emotionally weary and mentally worn out.

Laying in the hospital bed was the only position I knew for five days. I'll leave it to you to consider how certain necessities of life got accomplished. Immovable can change perspective. Looking back, I recall the items sitting atop the cart that rolls up to the bed. A bag of Peanut-Butter M&M's, a Styrofoam cup of ice water, and my Bible. Over those five days, hospital personnel consistently refilled the cup, I ate the entire contents of the orange bag – not the size that comes out of a vending machine, but the over-sized Costco bag – and I read and studied the Book of Joshua.

I have many explanations why I deserved the candy and had the right to consume every multi-colored piece, but it will not change the fact that it was unnecessary. The more favorable feast came from God's Word.

Each time I teach a Bible study, I invite the group to recite Jeremiah 15:16 with me. *When Your words came, I ate them; they were my joy and my heart's delight, for I bear Your Name, O Lord, God Almighty.* Reading and studying the Bible is consumption with great benefit.

A cow chews its cud twice for proper digestion. Cattle chews on average eight hours a day. Research teaches that they are ruminant animals – they have four compartments in their stomachs. The first compartment the food goes to is called the rumen.

As I began to read Joshua, I ruminated. I effectively chewed, consuming and digesting God's Word – pondering and meditating on the contents. As I ruminated, my emotions, my thoughts, and my heart were affected. God's Word brought me face-to-face with Jesus. We can't have an encounter with God and go unaffected. Yes, my expectations went unmet, but my hunger for the Lord was satisfied. And though I was physically weak, in pain, and immobile for five days, my inner strength was restored.

In Mark 1:30 a busy woman is knocked down with a fever. I assume this woman is the type to go with the flow. A hungry and tired group of people shows up, and it would be natural for her to welcome them into her home. But today, she's immobile, weakened from a fever; flustered and frustrated.

At the end of verse thirty, another use of *they* has my

attention. "…and they told Jesus about her."

KEY POINT: STRENGTH COMES WHEN OTHERS HAVE OUR BACKS

A face-to-face encounter with Jesus is not dependent on human interaction. However, our God is a relational God, and He loves to use people to connect people to His Son. There are times when weakness and weariness weigh us down and keep us from seeing Jesus. We need reminding, we need help, we need someone else. When *they* come to our rescue and lead us back to Jesus, we're strengthened because *they* have our back.

We use the idiom, *I have your back*, when we're willing and prepared to help, defend, and look out for another. The *I've-got-you* attitude isn't just for moral and emotional support. It's effective and a necessity for our spiritual well-being. Difficulties and dilemmas occur when the position reserved for Jesus is manned by another person or circumstance. If our eyes are off Jesus then we're weak, weary, and worn-out. He desires to lock eyes with you, not stare at your back. Strength comes when people have your back.

I experienced an abiding strength when I walked my cancer journey. And it was due to people having my back. It was as if a never-ending line of people followed me everywhere I went. Surgery, chemo, and radiation pushed me around, threatening my stance. But there were always people at my back ready to steady me. I was never alone. My people loved me well. When cancer knocked me down, *they* had my back.

I like to think in pictures and analogy. When I was a senior in high school, during spring break, half of the choir went on a tour. We began in Michigan, with our destination Colorado. One stop along the way was St. Louis. I remember it was a windy day as we stood at the base of the Gateway Arch, the monument to the westward expansion of our great nation.

A strong wind blew with immense force. As we stood at the corner of the arch, we were able to trust-fall onto what we couldn't see but what we knew was strong enough to have our backs. My people were the strong wind at my back when cancer knocked me over. With my people at my back, I was standing strong, face to face with Jesus.

They told Jesus about Simon's mother-in-law. Instead of getting in her face – *hey! Get up, we have company; you can rest* later. They had her back leaving the forefront available for Jesus.

When they told Jesus about her, *they* weren't informing Jesus why they couldn't smell food. In her weakness, *they* have her back, and they're helping to connect her to Jesus. Before *they* need dinner, Simon's mother-in-law needs a face-to-face encounter with Jesus.

KEY POINT: STRENGTH COMES WHEN JESUS COMES

Five beautiful words begin Mark 1:31. "So, He went to her..." Jesus went to her. Notice who initiates. Jesus does. Every single time. She didn't request His presence. She didn't extend an invitation – He showed up bedside without her awareness or involvement. Jesus comes out of compassion for her and a desire to meet her need, stepping into her current reality. He went to her because He loves her, whether she's standing strong or knocked down.

Picture this: He calmly enters her room, never breaking stride until he reaches the bedside. Her lighter complexion shows her flushed face. A low-grade temperature wouldn't knock this woman down, but she's burning up. Her eyes are glazed, and heat emanates from her body.

Some might think *they* should have called a doctor. Remember what *they* have seen and what *they* have heard as they followed Jesus. *They* call on the one who recently called them. Her core need is not physical. We all share the same primal need – a face-to-face encounter with Jesus.

Jesus went to her. Kneeling, He comes face-to-face with this sick woman. A man she's never met is in her bedroom, bedside, locking eyes with her. There's no earthly explanation or reasonable rationale why she shouldn't be agitated or anxious or fearful that a stranger is in her room. Mark 1:28 does say news about Him spread quickly over the whole region. It wasn't the news about Him that calms her. It's His peace that passes all understanding guarding her heart and her mind in this face-to-face encounter. (Philippians 4:7)

The same authority that caused men to heed His straightforward invitation to "Come, follow me" is the same gentle influence kneeling at her bedside. The exact power that caused evil to hush and flee at His command of "Be quiet, come out of him!" is silently holding her glazed gaze.

The end of Psalm 123:2 records, "...so our eyes look to the Lord, our God, till He shows us His mercy." A large picture hangs in our living room. Within the frame is a depiction of Good Friday. The artist captured many portrayals of that day – Jesus on the cross, demons hovering, darkness looming, angels attending, with death imminent. But, the eyes. A careful scrutiny shows eyes looking down on the cross – eyes of mercy, eyes of compassion – tender eyes looking down on the greatest demonstration of love mankind will ever know.

1 John 4:9 says, "This is how God showed His love among us: He sent His one and only Son into the world that we might live through Him." John 3:17 says, "For God did not send His Son into the world to condemn the world, but to save the world through Him." God's Son, the Messiah, Jesus, the Christ, has walked into a fevered woman's home; He entered her space, went to her, and looked at her with the same merciful, compassionate, and tender eyes that three years later will look down on Him in His darkest hour.

God loves her right where she is – in her knocked down state – but He loves her too much to leave her there. So, Jesus went to her, and continuing in Mark 1:31, "...took her hand..." First, He looked at her, and then He touched her – oh, He touched her. As mercy poured out of His tender eyes, did joy flood her soul? Was she consumed with peace? Where is her focus? Is it on the fever or on the one holding her hand?

What has your attention? What has you knocked down and in need of Jesus' touch? He comes to you, and His touch brings strength. I imagine He went to her, took her hand, and gently placed His other hand under her chin.

Psalm 3:3 says, "But your strength, O Lord, is round me, you are my glory and the lifter up of my head." [BBE – Bible in Basic English – translation] When we're down, Jesus comes, and He is our strength. When you're knocked down, Jesus comes, and He is the lifter of your head.

Jesus went to this woman because she was weak. Jesus touched this woman in her weariness. And there's more. Mark 1:31 continues, "...and helped her up." Jesus is the mighty miracle maker. All God's authority and healing power is in Jesus. He could have healed her from another room. He could have stood at the door and commanded her to come to Him. He could have healed her without a touch. But in His mercy, He went to a worn-out woman, touched her, and helped her up.

KEY POINT: STRENGTH DOES NOT MEAN STRIFE WILL DISAPPEAR

Strength comes from the presence of Jesus, not the absence of trouble. Strife does not retract, rescind, or revoke a face-to-face encounter with Jesus. Strength came once Jesus had her attention. Her eyes were off her struggle and on the Savior. Jesus helps her up and she's still fevered.

God helps those who help themselves is a HUGE lie straight from Satan. When we're knocked down, we're easily distracted to believe anything that sounds helpful or truthful. But just because it's said doesn't make it true. We are not capable of helping ourselves. If this woman can help herself, Jesus doesn't need to come. God sent His Son to save us because we can't save ourselves. On our own we're weak, weary, and worn-out. Jesus comes because we desperately need His touch and His help to strengthen us.

He went to her. He held her hand. He helped her up. And then Mark 1:31 says, "...the fever left her..." Physical healing came *after* her face-to-face encounter with Jesus. Her soul needed Jesus, her body needed healing. Jesus met both needs.

His compassion and mercy and grace drew her heart to Him, internally embedding His strength in her soul. His authority drove the fever away, restoring her physical strength. The end of Mark 1:31 records, "...and she began to wait on them."

KEY POINT: RESTORED STRENGTH BENEFITS OTHERS

Face-to-face encounters with Jesus allow us to stand strong. When strength is restored, we can effectively serve others. Simon's mother-in-law didn't waste any time getting back to her responsibilities. The text doesn't say she returned to her busy lifestyle. Rather, it says she began to wait on them. In the King James Version, it claims she *ministered unto them.*

Greek is the original language used here, and the word for ministered or waited on is *diakoneo,* which means deacon. The office of deacon or a diaconal minister are common positions held in churches today. They're elected or appointed to model servanthood – to provide sympathy and service.

Simon's mother-in-law had a face-to-face encounter with Jesus, was healed from the fever, and first on her mind was to serve others – she began to wait on them. *They* came to her house hungry and tired – weak, weary, and worn-out followers. We all have a *they* that unexpectedly show up in our life. How do you respond? Sympathy or apathy? Mercy or indifference?

This once-fevered woman chooses well. She is not her focus. Restored health brought strength to her body, but Jesus strengthened so much more. With her eyes still fixed on Jesus, she's able to see the needs of others. Now their need has her attention. And it's a chain-reaction.

KEY POINT: BUSYNESS KEEPS YOU OFF THE PORCH

My family has a summer place. There's approximately 2000 other families within the recreational park. Every lot and every home are under 1000 square feet. And almost every home has a deck or patio and a porch. As I write I'm inside, with our deck in view. Currently, no one is on the deck. But later today, my family arrives. Good things happen when we gather on the deck. Laughter, conversations, playing games, and eating food. If we remain busy inside, we miss the good things happening on our decks, patios, and porches.

Portions of Mark 1:32-34 say, "[32] That evening...people brought to Jesus all the sick and demon-possessed. [33] The whole town gathered at the door, [34] and Jesus healed many...He drove out many demons..."

A different sort of hungry and thirsty are gathered on Simon and Andrew's porch. *They* are hungry for the One that satisfies, thirsty for the only true source of living water, and they knew they could come to this porch and find the healing and wholeness Jesus offers.

Who's at your door? Can the hungry gather on your deck and be satisfied? Will their thirst for righteousness be quenched? The weary, weak, and worn out need a place to gather. Can they come to your door and encounter Jesus Christ?

Or, are you busy?

A few years back, a popular word could be found at craft fairs and on Target shelves. Bracelets and necklaces, tattoos and t-shirts had this one word sketched, etched, painted, carved, embroidered, chiseled, welded, burnt, and woven on its many canvases – a fad, charming many. Apparently, a need to be less complicated caused a stir, birthing the one-word mantra of *simplify*.

So, I wonder, does the piece of art simply declare it's time to clean, purge, and reorganize? Does displaying the word lessen the after-school activities? Were the bearers of this mantra encouraged to remove the haven't-worn-in-years sizes from the closet? If one-word brings about change, has the slogan delivered what it declares? I'm not convinced. Yes, a word, a mantra, can influence, but it holds no power to make necessary life changes.

It's easy to be confused – culturally, we deem the word *simplify* a mantra and then live busy lives. As I walk the aisles of Hobby Lobby and At Home or attend craft fairs, I haven't found *busy* as a one-word piece of artwork. Though it's not on the shelves of our favorite store, *busy* gets displayed in our lifestyles.

Busy keeps us off the porch. Busy doesn't have time for the deck. Then what will we do about the hungry and thirsty people in our communities? Satan does a splendid job at getting followers of Jesus believing busy is ok and accepting it as a lifestyle. The Deceiver has distracted us, ignoring our recent claim of the need to simplify, and settling for busy lives that have us weary, weak, and worn out. Busy believers need a face-to-face encounter with Jesus.

KEY POINT: HUNGER AND THIRST FOR RIGHTEOUSNESS

Busy has us depleted and drained of strength. We're weary, weak, and worn out. We believe busy gratifies, yet we're searching for sustenance and satisfaction amid the hectic and non-stop activity.

In Matthew chapter five, crowds gather alongside Jesus and His disciples. A mountainside is the scene, not a porch or a bedside, yet the weary, weak, and worn out are present. All are face-to-face with Jesus as He teaches and preaches.

In some Bibles, throughout the Gospels of Matthew, Mark, Luke, and John, the spoken words of Jesus are in red letters. Matthew Chapters five, six, and seven are mostly red. Jesus has things to say because His followers have things to learn. Jesus teaches and preaches to the hungry and thirsty. We're desperate for His instruction, His correction, His warning, and His message, and it provides us the strength we need to live holy lives.

In Matthew 5:6, Jesus says, "Blessed are those who hunger and thirst for righteousness, for they will be filled." Jesus doesn't wish this on His followers, nor does He simply hope it will happen. No! He declares it so.

Blessed are those also translates to *happy are those*. We must be careful we don't make assumptions on the meaning. Culturally, happy is joy, contentment, or satisfaction. Some equate financial gain as happiness. Others attach happiness to material possessions. Some believe blessing or happiness is something to pursue. Some think it's a good life or prestige. Others believe it's because you have good kids or a great job.

Kevin and I are parents to six. I gave birth to four, and we adopted two. As a mom, my kids have heard me say, "I don't pray for your happiness – I pray you know Jesus and live right." 3 John 4 says, "I have no greater joy than to hear that my children are walking in the truth." Walking refers to how people conduct themselves, regulating their life to God's ways. In this verse, the word for truth is the same word Jesus used when He said, "I am the way, the truth, and the life." (John 14:6)

I desire that my kids hunger and thirst for righteousness more than they pursue an education, claim a career, build a bank account, or reside on easy street. They can have the things that make them happy, but this momma will pray for their hearts before she wishes for their success.

When Jesus says, "Happy are those" or "Blessed are those" He's referring to those who love the Lord and love His Word – those who walk in the truth. They will be blessed and happy – based on His terms. Busyness keeps us distracted and searching for sustenance and satisfaction only righteousness gives. Pursuing righteousness and hungering to live a holy life stand strong.

We send the wrong message to our kids when we live busy. They believe overcommitted is acceptable. We teach them eating more meals in the SUV is the norm, while the dining room or kitchen table is for collecting the mail and completing homework. If the things on our calendars and color-coded agendas brings happiness, then why are so many followers of Jesus weary, weak, and worn out? What would happen if we stopped living busy lives and began living as Jesus intended and modeled?

An active life is a good life. In Mark 1:35, Jesus demonstrates what's necessary to properly live out a committed and full life-style. "...Jesus...went off to a solitary place, where He prayed."

- **He went off.** Busy has us flying off the handle, living crazy and chaotic life styles. Jesus went off – He departed, He stepped away, He took a breather, He took a break. Following His example, we need to step away from the distractions of an active life. Busy has us go off – verbal vomit on the ones we love. Busy encourages us to be busier, with no time to get away. Active has the sense to step away so we're not taken away by the crazy-busy.

- **He prayed.** We can't handle busy well; therefore, we should hand over our schedules to the Lord. Perhaps a new sign should be displayed above the calendar hanging on my refrigerator: Under New Management. Jesus prayed about His day. He went to God for strength. Yes, Jesus, the Son of God experienced weariness and weakness. Yes, He was worn-out. Jesus wore flesh and knew what it was to be physically hungry and thirsty, bodily weary and weak.

Jesus loved spending time with His Father. He spoke to Him and listened to Him and made it a priority, never allowing busy to take over His purpose.

Are you ready to satisfy your hunger and quench your thirst? In John 6:35, more red letters lead us to fulfillment. Jesus proclaimed, "I am the bread of life. He who comes to me will never go hungry, and he who believes in me will never be thirsty."

Hunger means needy. What's your need? Not your want – getting what we want makes us happy; having our needs met satisfies completely. Jesus satisfies our hunger and proclaims blessing for those who walk in truth and hunger for righteousness.

Thirsty means to long for the things that refresh, support, and strengthen our soul. According to Jesus, if we come to Him, we'll never be needy and if we believe in Him we're strengthened. Come means follow. Believe is total surrender.

Busy has us chasing satisfaction and surrendering to chaos, leaving us weary, weak, and worn-out. Being face-to-face with Jesus and living as He intends – satisfied and strong.

PONDER

deeply, carefully, and thoughtfully consider

1. Would you say you live a busy life or an active life?

2. The disciples left everything to follow Jesus. Since leaving doesn't imply an address change, carefully consider if there's anything in your life that hinders you from following Jesus.

3. Consider how often you hunger for Jesus to meet *the wants* more than *the needs* in your life.

PERSUADE

God's Word influences, encourages, and guides

1. In Mark 1:18 we read how the disciples left their business and followed Jesus. How can this action influence us as followers of Jesus?

2. Mark 1:24 shows us how Jesus confronts evil. Does this encourage you to face the distractions in your life? What can you do?

3. What three things did Jesus do as He came face-to-face with the fevered woman?

   a. He _____ to her
   b. He _____ her hand
   c. He _____ her up

   How can this help you when you're knocked down and need of strength?

PRACTICAL

applying Biblical Truth to present day

1. Look up Proverbs 31:17, how can you apply this in your life?

2. Write out Psalm 3:3.

   _____

   _____

   _____

   _____

   _____

   a. How does referring to the Lord as *the lifter of my head* strengthen you?

3. Read Matthew 5:6.

   a. What is righteousness?
   b. Are you hungry for it?
   c. Do you thirst for it?
   d. How are you challenged to live this out?

PERSONAL

inviting Jesus into your current reality

1. A busy woman in Mark 1:29-31 was knocked down with a fever. Only a face-to-face encounter with Jesus allowed her to stand strong.

   a. Has busyness zapped your strength?

   b. What needs to change?

   c. What can you do about it?

   d. What will you do about it?

2. Do you need to modify *busy* in your life?

3. How does busyness contribute to being weary, weak, or worn out?

2
strength for the HOPELESS

"He will keep you strong to the end..."
1 Corinthians 1:8

I'm grateful I live in the state shaped like a mitten. Ask me where I live in Michigan, and I'll hold up my left hand, palm facing out, thumb pulled in close toward the index finger but still slightly bent outward and point to the spot where my town is located. I'm not weird because anyone from Michigan does this.

South of where the thumb meets the base of the index finger is Frankenmuth, a popular tourist destination. I never tire driving through this town. In the past, I would often travel a certain backroad, passing a church. Its name is on the marquee, but it's also found as four free-standing letters. H-O-P-E stands tall near the landscaping at the side of the building.

Once when my daughter Christine and I were together, we noticed the P was knocked over. We chuckled and joked about the missing letter. Weeks later, I had reason to repeat the journey. Passing the church, I observed that same letter, still down.

How many followers of Jesus live the same way – a storm blows into their life and hope is disabled, damaged, or debilitated. Hopelessness happens and has us weary, weak, or worn-out.

After Jesus left Capernaum, where the busy woman lived, He travelled throughout Galilee, preaching and teaching and performing miracles. Mark 2:1-2 tells us Jesus returns to Capernaum and most likely back to

Simon's house. Because news about Jesus spread quickly, people gathered there. People, once again, heard about Jesus.

Mark 2:2 says, "So many gathered that there was no room left, not even outside the door." When I take personality profile assessments, and the preference is either introvert or extrovert, I lean on the extrovert side. Ok, lean might not be accurate – it's more fitting to say I'm totally standing near extrovert. I like being around people, meeting people, watching people, but I do not enjoy being crowded by people.

You will never find me shopping the day after Thanksgiving. Though I love New York City, I have no desire to visit Time's Square on New Year's Eve. I do, however, enjoy a crowd when cheering for the Detroit Tigers in their stadium – probably because everyone has his or her own seat.

The crowd gathered willy-nilly at this house in Capernaum has caused a furor – a fusion of excitement and disturbance. Folks are excited to see what everyone is talking about, while others are desperate for an up-close and personal position in hopes of receiving or witnessing a miracle.

Some women don't do well in situations of disorganization. I've seen the news stories when a bridal store has a massive sale. As women squeal hoping to get a deal, fabric flies while elbows and shoulders press. I don't get it. It makes more sense to shop when the chaos calms. As a self-declared clearance rack junkie, there's always a sale somewhere. Apparently, some like to follow the crowd.

In 1976 I was twelve years old. At that time, the Silverdome was home to the Detroit Lions. However, football didn't draw the crowd of which I was a part. Billy

Graham did. I recall loading the church bus with my dad and some friends from youth group that October afternoon. Members of our church choir, including my dad, joined hundreds of others in one massive choir during the evening Crusade. I remember looking for my dad from my seat near the top of the stadium. Thousands of people were gathered to hear Reverend Graham preach. As the crowd sang the expected hymn *Just as I Am* at the conclusion of the sermon, hundreds responded to Mr. Graham's invitation. They pressed in, shoulders rubbing and elbows bumping, to receive new life in Christ or a miracle of healing.

I was a part of the crowd that day, and from a seat near the top of the Silverdome in Pontiac, Michigan, I witnessed Jesus at work.

KEY POINT: JESUS DRAWS A CROWD

As I write this chapter, a few days have passed since Billy Graham's funeral. When I heard of his death, the memory of that 1976 Crusade and being a part of the crowd floods my mind. Mr. Graham drew many crowds, but it wasn't Billy people responded to – oh, it was him preaching, but it was God's sound message, that inspired people to make life-altering decisions. The Holy Spirit draws and woos a crowd. Rev. Graham – he was there to be used by God.

And the same Spirit of God that drew a crowd to Billy's crusades is who we read about in Mark 2:2 as people are drawn to a certain porch in Capernaum. A crowd has gathered – a crowd so big there was no room left inside the house or outside the door – shoulders rubbed, and elbows bumped to see and hear Jesus.

In large stadiums, obstructed view seats go empty

unless there's a play-off game for an athletic contest or a superstar's concert or a ceremony for an extraordinary celebration. After all, missing moments misses out on the full experience. On this crowded porch, the same people attempting to see Jesus are also obstructing the view of others seeing, hearing, and touching this one they've heard about.

The crowd on the porch was overflow from inside the house. For the people arriving last, others became their barricade, blocking and hindering them from seeing and hearing Jesus. Those in the obstructed view section might consider their situation hopeless.

Unless you're in the Harbin House – Sunday morning worship begins Saturday night. We had four kids in five years. Before Kevin was a pastor, we knew what it was like trying to get a family loaded into the van and walking into church without anyone crying or screaming. Cereal and the accompanying bowls and spoons were put on the table Saturday night. Outfits were pulled out of dressers and closets the night before and set out for convenience and ease and a better chance of leaving on time.

After Kevin completed his seminary degree and was serving his first pastoral assignment, he would leave the house before any of the children were awake. Well, truth is, we intentionally avoid each other, too. Over twenty years and two additional children later, we still see each other for the first time in the lobby of the church. (It's hard to argue when you don't talk or see each other.) On a rare occasion, there's a carry-over argument from Saturday to Sunday.

Though it happened years ago, I can still recall the memory as if it were yesterday. It was 10:25 a.m. and I was the song leader that Sunday. I took my seat on the platform waiting for the worship service to begin. My husband walked up the steps opposite me and took his seat. Generally, Kevin and I are very good at separating his role of pastor to family man. As he ascended the steps, I might have eye-rolled. When he took his seat, followed by the obvious prayer position, I may have exhaled in Darth Vader fashion.

Yes, I was clearly ready to lead our people in worship through song. As I was holding tightly to my bad attitude and preparing the speech I would later recite to Kevin with all the demonstrative emotion in all the right places, God was tapping on my heart.

I knew Kevin was taking the five minutes to prepare his pastoral heart to lead our congregation and preach God's Word. As Kevin was praying, God was about to break through my hurting heart. I felt hopeless. And it was obstructing my view of Jesus.

Jesus broke through the barricade and as if His fingers were under my chin, He opened my eyes to the crowd gathering in the sanctuary. Immediately, I heard a still small voice inquire, "How will they see Me if your attitude is in the way?" My tense shoulders settled, and the whisper continued, "And how can your husband freely preach My Word with your attitude in his way?" Hopelessness blocked my view of Jesus, but my attitude was responsible for the obstructed view of others.

At 10:28, I stood up, walked across the stage, sat next to my husband and said, "Don't look at me because I'll cry, just listen – Jesus told me I needed to come over and apologize. I'm sorry for last night. I'm sorry I was such a brat. Now I'm going back to my seat." After an inhale and exhale, I then said, "And Pastor Kevin, preach with fire!" I returned to my seat and readied my heart to lead the crowd through song, in praise of Jesus.

Yes, Jesus draws the crowd, but we must be aware of

when we're blocking and hindering others from clearly seeing Him. In Mark 2:2 it says, "...and [Jesus] preached the word to them." The ministry of Jesus continues, but those with an obstructed view can miss out on receiving and applying the complete message, leaving them in a hopeless state.

KEY POINT: NAVAGATE THE CROWD WELL

Hopeless people aren't easy people to be around. Often, we pretend not to notice them, even avoiding and ignoring them. And it's wrong. We must be aware of each person in the crowd. Matthew Henry, a Bible commentator, says the people gathered at this house in Mark Chapter two came to Jesus for cures, and others came out of curiosity. People today are no different – some are curious, and others are searching for cures.

For those who hope in the Lord, we have the treasure! We personally know the hope of glory. So, hopeless moments are a thing of the past, right?

Wrong! Knowing the hope of glory does not remove the possibility of facing seemingly hopeless situations. 1 Timothy 4:10 says, "...we have put our hope in the living God, who is the Savior of all, and especially of those who believe." And in 1 Peter 1:3 it says, "...In his [God's] great mercy he has given us new birth into a *living hope* through the resurrection of Jesus Christ..." Why would Peter mention hope if hopelessness isn't a part of the journey in following Jesus?

Hope lives today, because hopelessness threatens tomorrow. Jesus is our hope today and He'll remain our living hope tomorrow. In Mark 2:3, Jesus is preaching. As the crowd continues to gather, some men bring a hopeless man in hopes of seeing Jesus. We can't begrudge the crowd for not creating necessary space for the hopeless ones to get a front row seat, but we can use this situation to teach us to more efficiently navigate the crowds around us.

"Some men came, bringing to him a paralytic, carried by four of them." (Mark 2:3) A small crowd brings a hopeless man to the larger crowd. These men navigate the crowd well because they don't allow the crowd to dissuade their objective: Get their hopeless friend to Jesus. The paralytic is without hope – his legs can't get him to Jesus and a crowd obstructs his view of Jesus. However, this hopeless situation doesn't mean that Living Hope isn't present. Thank God his four friends are full of hope. They trusted in the Living Hope when his hopes were dashed.

Using Mark 2:3-4, these four friends teach us three points to navigate the crowd well.

- Prepare
- Persist
- Prevail

Prepare: These four men prepared ahead to bring the paralytic to Jesus. Mark doesn't tell us, but we can assume they knew about Jesus, believed Jesus, and trusted Jesus because this small group came looking for Him, knowing He could meet the paralytic's need. Maybe they were present in the synagogue, heard Jesus teach, and witnessed Him call evil out of the man. It's possible they were part of another crowd as Jesus was outside Capernaum. Maybe they saw others receive healing, and it influenced them to get their paralytic friend and go find where Jesus had gone. Their preparation proves they were hopeful. They believed in this Living Hope and had faith He could restore a hopeless man.

Persist: These four friends didn't lose hope at the edge of the crowd. Yes, their view was obstructed. Yes, the crowd was a barricade. They didn't allow obstructions and barricades to deter their hope. Instead, they planned a detour. Navigating a crowd well, involves executing a plan when that plan appears hopeless. Mark 2:4 says, "Since they could not get him to Jesus because of the crowd, they made an opening in the roof above Jesus and, after digging through it, lowered the mat the paralyzed man was lying on."

Despite the crowd, they persisted. Perseverance is a steady persistence with a purpose. Before they made an opening in the roof, they had to get the friend and his mat up on the roof. They're already sweating and worn-out, yet they persist. Strength comes through persistence. Strength comes through a face-to-face encounter with Jesus, and they desperately desire their paralyzed friend meet Jesus.

Hope for his healing had them continuing with a plan to get him to Jesus. Weary, weak, and worn-out, they become a four-man pulley system. Synchronized movements are planned actions. Persistence and hope supported the makeshift, human elevator.

Prevail: These four men prevailed because they overcame obstacles and barricades for their friend. Their persistence on the roof produced a commotion, causing some in the crowd to look up. I'm sure this prevailing plan caused some in the crowd to be annoyed and disturbed, even to the point of petulance. *How dare they interrupt Jesus. The nerve! What makes them think their friend needs Jesus more than us? We were here first. What are they doing up there? Can't they hear Jesus is talking?*

Though opposition is present, these four men prevail through their hope in Jesus, spurring them to bring their hopeless friend to Him.

The four friends didn't initiate a face-to-face encounter with Jesus for the hopeless man, God did, because He's always working ahead of us. These four men carried Jesus, but God carried them. "Many are the plans in a man's heart, but it is the Lord's purpose that prevails." (Proverbs 19:21) This small group of men responded to the prevailing work of God.

KEY POINT: MAKE SURE OUR PLAN IS GOD'S PURPOSE

As the paralytic was being lowered through the roof, the crowd saw a paralyzed man on a mat while Jesus had eyes for the faith of four men in action. Luke's account says they landed him "...right in front of Jesus." (Luke 5:19) A face-to-face encounter with the Living Hope ensued. Both Mark and Luke record, "When Jesus saw their faith..."

Every heart filling the room and every heart crowding outside the door came to Jesus with a personal plan. Some plan for healing. Others plan on learning. Some come to stand at a distance to catch a glimpse at what they've heard. In this crowd, there are plans to be skeptical, plans to evaluate, plans to follow; there may even be a plan to disrupt and dissuade.

People came hoping their plan would unfold; Jesus came with purpose. Jesus came to this house to unburden the weary, strengthen the weak, and refresh the worn-out. Since He is the same yesterday, today, and forever, He comes to unburden, strengthen, and refresh us, as well. This paralytic man has a hope he'll walk. God has a purpose for this man to walk by faith. Oh, to be a follower who plans according to God's purposes.

In Isaiah 49:16, the prophet named for this Book in the Bible declares one of God's hope-filled promises to those who are in relationship with Him. "See, I have engraved you on the palms of my hands…" In other versions, this word, *engraved*, is changed to marked, written, graven, and inscribed. At times, I better understand things using analogy. When I envision God's hand, I see a large, open palm with graffiti-style names tattooed on it.

I believe every tattoo should tell a story. Mine do. Since turning 40, I started considering one. Five years later I received the first of two. Just above my outer, right ankle is a sun. Firmly connected to the sun are twelve beams, six small and six large. The sun represents Jesus, the Light of the World. Each larger beam characterizes me, my husband, and our four older children with coordinating birthstone colors.

I'm not one to do anything because everyone else is doing it. I wasn't pressured, coerced, or made to get permanently inked. Though I was in mid-life, it was a certain crisis that highly influenced my decision to get my family tattoo. Four months later, God opened doors we thought were closed, and we adopted our youngest two children. Obviously, that required another tattoo.

On the top of my right foot, appearing to fall from the sun, are two shooting stars. The blue one signifies Jaylen's birth month, with the purple one representing Sukanya's. My forever family is forever inscribed onto my leg.

According to Ephesians 1:5, when we come into a relationship with God, through His Son, Jesus, we're adopted into His family. Isaiah 62:2 says, "…you will be called by a new name…" And this same prophet declared all who are in God's forever family have their names engraved on the palm of His hand.

And this promise should encourage God's family members that His plan for His followers has purpose. Confusion and disappointment occur when we expect God to infuse His purpose into our man-made plan. Like this crowd, we have many plans. Do our plans allow for God's purpose? A crowd looks on as four men are affirmed in their faith. A crowd is influenced by faith in action. As Living Hope speaks to a hopeless paralytic, "Son, your sins are forgiven," confusion, frustration, indignation, annoyance, and offense join the crowd. Ignorance keeps us uninformed.

Jesus meets needs, not expectations. The paralytic needed a face-to-face encounter with Jesus more than he needed his legs to work. The four men prepared, persisted, and prevailed because they had a plan, an expectation – get their broken friend to Jesus. God had a purpose – to meet his greatest need.

Though our plans and expectations vary, God's purpose for all is the same – He sent His Son into the world to save people from the penalty of sin. We're sinners in need of saving – we need redemption, we need rescue, we need forgiveness, we need grace – and Jesus is God's purposeful solution to our need.

While the paralytic lies still on his mat, Jesus saves him; Jesus forgives his sin. Be careful not to miss what Jesus calls the broken man "son". [Mark 2:5] Jesus greets him as a family member. But it's more – Jesus declares the broken man a part of God's family. Before Jesus proclaims him forgiven, He declares him accepted.

KEY POINT: BEWARE, INTELLIGNECE CAN LEAD TO IGNORANCE

Acceptance and forgiveness from Jesus toward the paralytic and his friends brought confusion, frustration, indignation, annoyance, and offense to some ignorant witnesses in the crowd.

Mark 2:6 records, "Now some teachers of the law were sitting there, thinking to themselves..." Let's pause. Teachers of the law, or scribes, were intelligent, educated men. They examined difficult topics and researched answers to challenging questions to the religious, Jewish practices. These scholars interpreted Jewish religious law – it was their life's work. Having undisputed sway over the people, whatever the Scribes taught was taken to mind...until Jesus came to earth.

In Matthew 5:17, as He's preaching, Jesus says, "Do not think that I have come to abolish the Law or the Prophets; I have not come to abolish them, but to fulfill them." He went on to say all that was written in the Law is expected to be accomplished – the teaching and obeying of the commandments. However, the teachers of the law were skeptics and critics. They, too, followed Jesus, hoping to find fault and error in His preaching and teaching.

And here they sat, listening carefully, not missing one beat, to a man who hadn't followed their same educational plan. They, too, heard about this Jesus. It's possible authority may have sent them, but curiosity accompanied them. The stir Jesus caused, combined with their intelligence and education, would have these scribes on high alert.

The scribes had a front row seat as the paralytic made his grand entrance and landed *right in front of Jesus*. And, according to Mark, they began thinking to themselves. (In Mark 2:8 we understand how Mark could record what they were thinking.) These scribes came to the gathering skeptical and maintained their cynical attitude. As Jesus saw faith in action, they were blinded by ignorance. We often associate ignorance with stupidity, when it's accurately defined as unaware. These scribes have had so much education, they were ignorant when revelation had their attention. God was revealing Himself through Jesus. The scribes knew God through the law. Through Jesus, God would reveal His love for humanity. The scribes should have been the ones to connect what the prophets from the Old Testament said regarding God's ultimate redemption plan. But all their education had them blinded to Jesus being the fulfillment of those prophecies.

Many who get saved never grow up, content to know a lot about God but stop short from growing in their relationship with God. They recite Bible verses, creeds, and prayers. They sit in their self-reserved spot every Sunday morning. They volunteer in leadership roles, knowing well the polity and organizational structure of their churches. Like the scribes, they're front and center when faith is put into action, but they're ignorant to connect the spiritual dots. Perhaps they, too, think to themselves.

My dad retired at an early age from his career at Ford Motor Company. A few years later, he answered the call to ministry, and at 55 he became a pastor. My dad tells of one time he was standing and singing in his usual manor – perhaps too boisterous for some preferences but never disruptive or spiritually unacceptable. At times, he would step away from the lectern, or podium, for the Scripture reading. One day a long-time church member said to him, "It annoys me when you block my view." Ignorance.

My husband tells of the time he pastored a small rural church and one of the leaders said, "I don't understand why you always quote that book." She was referring to the Bible. Ignorance.

An accusing thought was flanked by two unspoken questions. (Mark 2:7) "Why does this fellow talk like that? He's blaspheming! Who can forgive sins but God alone?" Out of ignorance the scribes internalized their accusations. In Isaiah 43:25, the prophet says, "I – yes, I alone – will blot out your sins..." (New Living Translation) So, yes, scribes, the prophet you're familiar with provided the answer to this question. The problem is they don't believe Jesus is God's Son. They're trusting intelligence to explain something that requires a measure of faith.

Jesus isn't a *fellow*; He's God with skin on. And His *talk like that* is not blasphemy – it's Godly. Their accusation is born out of educated intelligence. When it comes to the things of God, revelation trumps education. Shaping their minds kept their hearts from seeing the Word who became flesh. (John 1:14) Their eyes only saw what their intelligence convinced them was true. Therefore, they did not recognize Him or receive Him as God. (John 1:10-11)

Jesus came to open the eyes of our hearts, but when we're focused on filling our minds with more things about God, we become ignorant to the plans and purposes of God.

KEY POINT: WE CAN'T KNOW THE MIND OF GOD, BUT HE SEES OURS

In Mark 2:8 we learn Jesus knew in his spirit what they were thinking *in their hearts*. Their education and intelligence didn't just stay in their minds – it filtered to their hearts. And our hearts get affected by our thoughts. The word Jesus uses for *heart* denotes the center for all physical and spiritual life. The word *soul* could also be used, meaning the center and seat of spiritual life.

Proverbs 23:7 (BBE) says, "For as the thoughts of his

heart are, so is he..." The scribes were trusting the knowledge stored in their minds, and this confrontation between Jesus and the paralytic internally unsettled them. But, Jesus didn't come to first change minds, He came to save souls. 1 Corinthians 1:11 says, "...no one knows the thoughts of God except the Spirit of God." The Spirit of God controlled the flesh part of Jesus, but being God-with-skin-on, Jesus read the minds of the scribes, leaving the teachers of the law speechless throughout the rest of this face-to-face encounter.

But Jesus Has words for them. In Mark 2:8-10 Jesus responds to their unspoken thoughts. They were accusing a man of taking the role of God. But Jesus was acting in the place He has occupied since before the world began. His rightful response to their questions could have been, "Because I'm God." However, Jesus isn't snarky, but He is clever.

- Why are you thinking these things?
- Which is easier to say?

Imagine the confusion within and amongst the scribes. He doesn't wait for their answer as He slips in the second question plus a revelation. [9]"Which is easier to say to the paralytic, 'Your sins are forgiven' or to say, 'Get up, take your mat and walk'? [10] But that you may know that the Son of Man has authority on earth to forgive sins..." Jesus wasn't looking for answers. His questions meant to challenge their thinking for a change of heart.

With the scribes stuck in their seats and the crowd looking on, a paralytic has a face-to-face encounter with Jesus. The Voice of Truth turned away from the scribes and looked directly at the paralytic and continued

speaking. "I tell you, get up, take your mat and go home."
(Mark 2:11)

KEY POINT: GETTING UP, STANDS STRONG

The paralytic lay at a crossroads. Jesus told him to get up, but He didn't lend a hand. The paralytic had a choice: Stay put or get up. What would happen if he stayed put? Nothing, his life would remain the same...no change, no hope, no miracle.

Jesus had a miracle for this man – but the man needed to walk by faith before he took that first step. Let me be clear, the man didn't need his legs to work to know hope and live at peace and have joy. The miracle doesn't bring hope; Jesus alone brings hope to the hopeless. If He chooses to perform a miracle, that's His prerogative. Followers of Jesus must be careful we don't hope for a miracle more than we desire an encounter with the Mighty Miracle Maker.

The paralytic is in a face-to-face encounter with Jesus, and a miracle awaits him. But he needs to first get up. Mark 2:12 says, "He got up..." He's never stood before. He has no idea if his legs will hold his body weight. Did he wobble? Was he weak? I don't believe so. *He got up* is the same Greek word the angel used at the empty tomb when he declared *He has risen*. (See: Matthew 28:6, Mark 16:6, and Luke 24:6)

The call to *Get up!* is accompanied with the strength to accomplish the assignment. What is your *get up* call? Get up and forgive? Get up and pray? Get up and trust? Get up and witness? Get up and invite? Get up and confront? Get up and stop – stop the gossip, stop the worry, stop the negativity, stop the bad habit, stop doubting? Then, get up and obey, and you'll be standing strong.

The next call from Jesus to the paralytic is *take your mat*. The former resting place represents his comfort zone and designates his safety and security. It's the one thing he consistently trusted in. Jesus loved this man as he lay on the mat and He loves him as he's standing on it. But Jesus loves Him too much to leave him there.

Jesus is now the man's comfort, for he can completely trust Jesus to keep him safe and secure. For the man to pick up the mat, he'll need to step off the mat. To step off the mat, he'll need to trust Jesus.

Jesus didn't call anyone else to participate in this miracle – only the paralytic. We must remember, there is always someone else in need of a personal face-to-face encounter with Jesus. When Jesus performs a miracle, it affects more than the recipient – people are uplifted when they witness and hear what Jesus does in our life. This paralytic stepped off, bent over, and picked up the mat. He now carries what he no longer needs.

Then Jesus said, "Go home." And the man *walked out in full view of them all*. As this portrayal of strength and demonstration of faith walked out, hope filled the crowd.

Consider what happens if we don't get up and obey the call of Jesus. Will you get up, so they can see Jesus?

KEY POINT: HOPING IN JESUS, TRUSTS JESUS

Standing up gives us hope. Stepping off the mat and walking by faith requires a wholehearted trust in Jesus. Some followers of Jesus remain on the mat – oh, they've followed the command to *get up*, their hope and their eternal home are secure through Jesus, but they remain stuck on their faith journey. Discontentment, discouragement, fear, worry, and frustration are constant companions.

Jesus says get off the mat, walk by faith, trust in Him. In John 15, Jesus teaches He is the vine and His followers are the branches. His command is, "Remain in me…" (John 15:4) Followers of Jesus cannot simultaneously remain on the mat and stay connected to the vine.

After Rev. Billy Graham preached and while the massive crowd sang that familiar hymn, I watched as hundreds of people swarmed the makeshift altar. Souls were saved, hearts were changed, and hope was born as people were challenged to place their trust in Jesus. No one remained at the altar, but I wonder how many left, still stuck on their mats.

We've been inspired by sermons, renewed on retreats, convicted to change at a conference – we've done our time at the altar, committed to the call to *get up*. We have high hopes our life will be different, and it will be – if we wholeheartedly trust in Jesus. We can't step back on the mat if we never lay it down. When we're weary, weak, and worn-out, we need to assess where we're standing. If we're back on the mat, we're not fully trusting Jesus. Like the paralytic who no longer needed his mat we, too, only need to trust Jesus for all our next steps.

Hope and trust are good friends. As we walk by faith, we have hope in the One who calls us to get up and get off our mats. A face-to-face encounter with the Living Hope gave hope to a weary, weak, and worn-out man.

KEY POINT: A SEALED SOUL STANDS STRONG

Colossians 1:27 says, "…Christ in you, the hope of glory." The author of hope, the Messiah, God's Son dwells in humanity – redemption makes our heart, His home. What a mystery! Praise God, Jesus Christ heals and seals souls.

2 Corinthians 1:21-22 says, "[21] Now it is God who makes both us and you **stand firm** in Christ. He anointed us, [22] **set his seal** of ownership on us, and put his Spirit in our hearts as a deposit, guaranteeing what is to come." [emphasis mine]

God set His seal on our hearts. Followers of Jesus have been marked with a seal. This literally means a security from Satan. Not only are we engraved on the palm of His hand, but our souls are sealed. Leaning on Jesus is safe and secure from all alarms. Hoping in Jesus stands firm. Living for Jesus stands strong and is mandatory for those marked with His seal.

KEY POINT: STANDING STRONG, STANDS AMAZED

Mark 2:12 says, "...This amazed everyone, and they praised God, saying, 'We have never seen anything like this!" With working legs and a sealed soul, this man walked out in full view of everyone. The crowd witnessed what Jesus had done. This word *amazed* means to throw out of position or displace. They were thrown into wonderment and astounded at what they witnessed. Minds that were previously thinking are now blown away.

When was the last time your mind was blown by Jesus? Are you astounded by His acts of mercy and grace? When you hear a testimony of Jesus at work in someone else's life, are you thrown into wonderment? Do you stand amazed in the presence of Jesus? You should! When followers of Jesus are standing strong they look for His wonder-working power and amazing grace.

According to Mark 2:12, everyone was amazed. Every. Single. Person. No one is left out of everyone. The doubters, the confused, the frustrated, the scribes, the four friends – everyone was astonished that a paralyzed man got up, picked up his mat, and walked out in full view of them all.

The same crowd, who moments earlier stood shoulder-to-shoulder, now parted like the Red Sea as a paralytic walked out of the house. Jesus could have quietly performed the miracle and kept on preaching, but then, how could the weary, weak, and worn-out be strengthened? They needed to see this walking miracle.

After the man leaves, they weren't flocking to Jesus begging and pleading for their own miracle. Instead, they praised God. The original word is doxazo – to honor, glorify, and render it excellent. The man's sealed soul and healed legs were used to strengthen the crowd. And in their strength, they praised God, keeping their focus on Jesus. The hopeless became hopeful when their eyes were on Jesus.

All who are weary, weak, and worn-out need a face-to-face encounter with Jesus, not for what He can do, rather for who He is – Jesus, the Savior, our Living Hope.

PONDER

deeply, carefully, and thoughtfully consider

1. Think about a time when you were hopeless.

   a. How did you respond?
   b. How did others respond to your situation?
   c. If anything, what could you have done differently to know hope?

2. Carefully consider how your thoughts can lead to hopelessness. Is this helpful or hurtful to your faith journey?

3. What does it mean to you when Jesus says, "Remain in me." (John 15:4)

PERSUADE

God's Word influences, encourages, and guides

1. How do these verses encourage you regarding hope?

   a. 1 Peter 1:3
   b. 1 Timothy 4:10
   c. Isaiah 49:16
   d. Psalm 33:18
   e. Lamentations 3:19-23

2. Mark 2:3-4 teaches three points to influence us in bringing our hopeless friends to Jesus. How can these points encourage and guide you?

   a. Prepare

   b. Persist

   c. Prevail

PRACTICAL

applying Biblical Truth to present day

1. How do these passages of Scripture secure hope in your heart?

   a. Isaiah 62:2
   b. Ephesians 1:5
   c. Psalm 130:5

2. Read Psalm 62. Find at least three things you can apply to a hopeless situation today.

3. According to Mark 2:11, name the three things Jesus told the paralytic to do so he could stand strong. Do each of the points give you hope? How?

   a.
   b.
   c.

PERSONAL

inviting Jesus into your current reality

1. Write a prayer or a letter to God inviting Him into a hopeless situation or thanking Him for His tender, loving care through a hopeless situation.

3
strength for the
OUT OF CONTROL

"Their Redeemer is strong...He will vigorously defend
their cause so that he may bring rest..."
Jeremiah 50:34

Hockey moms, soccer dads, bleacher creatures at a basketball game – everyone who's ever sat at a sporting event for their kid has watched a parent lose control. It's not pretty. The fans are annoyed, the refs are blowing whistles, and their child is humiliated – again. Out of control persons have practiced their performance; therefore, it's rarely an isolated incident. Many communities have experienced devastating results from athletic contests gone wrong due to an out-of-control mom or dad.

News magazine shows like *Dateline*, *48 Hours*, and *20/20* highlight tragic storylines. Producers make sure we're hooked at the beginning of the show by giving us pertinent facts that occurred prior to the tragedy. And then the TV reporter interviews those caught in the aftermath. Most every episode involves ruthless, senseless, and horrifying behavior from an out-of-control individual.

Though I'm not entertained by these shows, I do collect them on the DVR. I glean lessons on humanity – the depravity, and the decency, in mankind. I don't watch to get sucked in to other people's drama; rather, I'm curious what causes people to snap and inquisitive about the ones who persevere.

Most folks who get out of control have a threshold and unique triggers that bring out the uncontrolled. It's also true that each narrative necessitates a backstory. In Mark Chapter five, we're introduced to an out-of-control man. If this were a current event, every network would be vying for the opportunity to tell his story. Three gospel accounts tell the man's tale, yet, they all leave out the backstory leading up to his current reality. Networks would lose ratings; however, Jesus gains followers through the telling of this story.

Mark begins Chapter five with location information. *They* sail across a lake to the region of the Gerasenes, which is near an isolated burial ground. Unless you're Jesus and a divine appointment is scheduled, this is a place most people would avoid. Notice, *they* accompany Him.

KEY POINT: FOLLOWERS FOLLOW WHERE JESUS LEADS

Jesus leads, and *they* follow. Hours before, Jesus boarded a boat, His disciples followed, and they began to cross to the other side of the lake. As they sailed, Jesus napped, and suddenly a furious squall – literally, a mega, violent wind – hovered over them and the waves broke over the boat. In other words, the weather started getting rough, the tiny ship was tossed.

If not for the courage of the fearless crew...wait. *They* were a fear-filled crew. Veteran fishermen were caught off-guard when the weather became out-of-control. The waves made them weary. The wind caused them to become weak. The weather had them worn-out. And Jesus naps.

If Jesus leads, why would He steer them into a squall? It's because followers of Jesus learn to trust Him and gain strength when they face unexpected storms. Jesus has a divine appointment on the other side (Mark 4:35). He knows this, but He didn't tell His followers. *They* must trust where Jesus leads. *They* must trust Jesus even when He appears to be unaware of what's brewing. Yes, Jesus is napping, but He's fully aware of where He steered His followers.

The storm diverted their attention. Now they're no longer focused on the directions Jesus gave. Mark 4:38 tells us they woke Jesus up and with accusation said, "...don't you care..." We must be careful when storms happen along our faith journey. Through trial and trouble and tragedy, we'll suffer weariness, encounter weakness, and become worn-out. And we'll think Jesus is taking a nap and He doesn't care.

KEY POINT: THE CURRENT STORM IS NOT THE LAST STORM

Oh, we do not like to talk about or think about future struggles. But haven't you lived long enough to know you can't stop a storm, avoid a storm, or wish a storm away? Through every torrent, Jesus cares – He's with us before the winds blow, when the waves crash, and as we're dealing with the debris and pieces left in the wake of the storm. The question is, what did you learn from the current storm that will help you when the next commotion comes?

They witnessed Jesus rebuke the wind and the waves (Mark 4:39). With an authoritative word, all went quiet. Jesus dialed down the wind and calmed the waves. Jesus may not stop the waves from crashing into our boat, but He promises to be our peace as the storm rages.

And *they* needed the storm in Mark Chapter four

because they were about to face a storm of different proportions on the other side. Often, things on the other side are quite different. Fiction often narrates about opposing sides – famous movies and books tell of the girl from the other side of the tracks or the boy from *that* part of town. People act differently, live differently, respond differently, and look differently.

In the chamber of the United States House of Representatives, court houses, city offices, and within denominations there's opposition due to the other side. At athletic contests, the opposing team always sits on the other side. Even in neighborhoods, people live on the other side of the street.

Trial, trouble, and tragedy occur on the other side, making us weary, weak, and worn out. We need the strength only Jesus offers when storms brew and blow into our lives. When He leads us into the unknown, it should comfort us that He is never surprised by what we'll find on the other side.

Mark 5:2 says, "When Jesus got out of the boat..." Once again, Jesus takes the lead. "...a man with an evil spirit came from the tombs to meet him." Evil approaches Jesus – but Deity isn't shocked. This isn't the first time evil approached Jesus. Evil has freedom to roam earth – Jesus, wearing flesh, is in evil's domain. However, even though Satan tried, evil never dominated Jesus. (See Matthew 4:1-11; Mark 1:12-13; and Luke 4:1-13.)

KEY POINT: EVIL IS STRONG, GOD IS STRONGER

The power of evil is proven through this demon-possessed man. Mark 5:3-5 describes his disturbing existence:

- He lived in the tombs
- He broke free of hand chains
- He broke free of foot irons
- No one was strong enough to subdue him
- Night and day, he would roam the tombs and hills
- Night and day, he would cry out
- Night and day, he would cut himself with stones

"When he saw Jesus from a distance, he ran and fell on his knees in front of him." (Mark 5:6) An out-of-control, demon-possessed man has eyes for Jesus. What compelled him to run to Jesus? What caused him to land on his knees in front of Jesus?

Any face-to-face encounter with Jesus begins with God's initiative. His Spirit woos and invites. Across the globe, at hundreds of Billy Graham Crusades, thousands of people responded to God's call on their heart as they walked to the makeshift altar. At the church I was raised in, folks knelt at the circular altar rail as the Holy Spirit wooed them forward. And here, on the other side, the same Spirit of God initiates, and an out-of-control man falls on his knees in front of Jesus near the seashore.

A battle of strength ensues. Evil held this man captive, but Jesus captivated the man. Though evil has a tight grip on him, he has his hope set on Jesus.

He shouted at the top of his voice, "What do you want with me, Jesus, Son of the Most-High God?' In the original language, *megas* and *phone* are the Greek words used for a loud voice. His guttural cry sounded like it came through a megaphone as he pleaded, "Swear to God that you won't torture me!" (Mark 5:7).

I wonder what the disciples are thinking as this crazy man shouts at Jesus on a dark beach. As we consider his out-of-control clamoring, pause and reflect on the last time you shouted at God. Has God received exclamations of frustration from you? Have howls of anger reached His ears? What about bellows of blame, roars of doubt, shrieks of impatience, cries of grief, or screams of pain?

Can Jesus handle all the shouting and exclaiming? The fast answer is, yes. But I think we're good at explaining our exclaiming when the truth is we're only yelling to excuse the rant. Circumstances have us weary, weak, and worn-out, zapped of strength and susceptible to becoming out of control.

Yes, there are times we're gripped by depths of grief and pain initiated by horrendous, hurtful, and harmful things. Sharing these deep grievances with God is acceptable, necessary, and beneficial to our relationship with Him. But there's a difference in communicating deep pain with your Father and spewing accusations at God in an out-of-control temper tantrum from a weary, weak, and worn-out follower.

God is omniscient, having complete and unlimited knowledge, awareness, and understanding. He perceives all things; therefore, He knows the depths of our hearts. He knows our pain. He's never surprised when we convey who hurt us, what harms us, or the horrendous acts committed against us. He knows, He always knows. It behooves followers of Jesus to remember this; otherwise, we're deceived to believe we need to inform Omniscience we're hurting as if He's unaware.

According to Mark, no one was strong enough to subdue this out-of-control man. He couldn't be tamed or restrained. Untamed and unrestrained are out-of-control.

Years ago, I remember sitting on my kitchen floor, spent, from the performance I had just executed. The audience was my three-year-old daughter and two-year-old and three-month-old sons. It's a real good thing they have no memory of that day. I vividly recall yelling at my two-year-old to stop crying. Yelling doesn't quite capture the explosion emitting out of me. It was somewhere between screaming and hollering. When a 28-year-old woman expects a two-year-old to stop acting like a toddler, that's out-of-control. Christine looked at me like I had grown a second head, and then she turned and walked away. If she was older, it's possible an eye-roll would have accompanied her retreat.

We must recognize what out of control looks like in our lives. If movies, works of fiction and fantasy, news magazine stories, or that crazy parent at our kid's athletic contest determine our definition of out of control, we'll struggle to recognize it in ourselves and never acknowledge we're prone to its power over us.

If the disciples only saw a naked, frenzied man screaming and shouting on the beach as their definition of out of control, then they won't acknowledge where the storm had taken them moments earlier. Redefining evil helps. Yes, it's massacre and mayhem. Certainly, it's terrorism and tyranny. Absolutely, it's diabolical and demonic. But, if that's our only perspective, then most of us would say we either don't have the capacity for evil or we're not affected by it.

KEY POINT: EVIL SPELLED BACKWARD IS LIVE

What if we defined evil as anything that has us live backward from God's ways? God says to love, but we choose to hate – that's evil. God says to honor your father and mother, but as kids, we dishonored their authority – that's evil. God says, not to gossip, but we flap our lips about one another – that's evil. God says, no coveting, but we want what she has – that's evil.

And evil lives backward. Only Jesus can turn evil around. The strength God offers and extends turns out-of-control disobedience, out-of-control gossip, out-of-control anger, out-of-control covetousness, out-of-control relationships – all out-of-control behavior gets turned around. Only a face-to-face encounter with Jesus has us live as He intends – turned around and away from evil.

In Mark 8:33, Jesus speaks a well-known rebuke. "Get behind me, Satan." When Jesus said this to Peter, He wasn't calling him Satan. He was turning His follower around. Peter was living backward. Jesus went on to say, "You do not have in mind the things of God, but the things of men." Peter's passion and motive was to defend Jesus. But Jesus doesn't need our defense. He calls for our obedience and trust.

When our passions take over, we cease wholeheartedly following Jesus. Oh, we're still His followers, but when something or someone other than Jesus has our attention, we're backward and need to be turned around.

The shouts on the beach emanated from evil, not the man. He needed to be freed from evil, and Jesus holds the power to do just that. Evil controls the man, but Jesus controls the outcome. First, we must recognize and acknowledge what has this man out-of-control.

In Mark 5:8, Jesus confronts evil. "Come out of this man, you evil spirit." In the King James Version, evil is referred to as *unclean*. The original word for *spirit* is pneuma – meaning the soul – that which makes us feel, think, and decide. Unclean feelings, unclean thoughts, and unclean decisions overtook the man, and Jesus confronts this evil and calls it out of the man. Mark 5:8 implies Jesus had the first word. "For Jesus had said to him, 'Come out of this man, you evil spirit!" Jesus ordered, demanded, authorized evil to leave the man, not the premises. Then evil begged Jesus not to torture him. (Mark 5:7)

Mark 5:9 says, "Then Jesus asked him, 'What is your name?" Jesus isn't making introductions on the beach. He's showing His followers He has authority over evil. When evil first spoke words, it used the pronoun *me*. (Swear to God that you won't torment *me*.) However, as we continue in Mark 5:9, evil went from *me* to *we*. "...My name is Legion, for we are many." A legion is a squad of over 6,000 soldiers. Basically, Legion is saying, "*We* infiltrated, and *we* took control of this man."

The disciples see a man. Jesus sees a legion of evil. The disciples see an out-of-control man. Jesus sees a man held captive. The disciples hear a man shouting at Jesus. Jesus hears evil tormenting the man. But, evil is scared to death because evil knows Jesus has the power and authority to turn evil around.

Evil understands that though it possessed this man, it cannot stronghold Jesus. Evil went from shouting at Jesus to begging Him to not use torture. The battle waged on.

As the man fell at the feet of Jesus, evil confessed Deity (Mark 5:6). Isaiah prophesied every knee would bow and every tongue would swear and say righteousness and strength are found only in the Lord (Isaiah 45:23-24). And Paul said, "...at the name of Jesus every knee should bow... and every tongue confess that Jesus Christ is Lord..." (Philippians 2:10-11).

Jesus desired this man live and that evil be vanquished. Jesus desired this man truly bow his knee and in his own voice confess, "Jesus is Lord." But first, this man must be rescued from the clutches of evil. Jesus is his rescue and evacuation plan.

KEY POINT: RESCUE SAVES US FROM DANGER

In Mark 5:10 evil begs Jesus, and it's not just a one-time plea. Rather, again and again, evil begs not to be sent out of the area. Interesting – this region is a comfort zone for Legion. In Mark 5:1 Jesus led His disciples to this region of the Gerasenes. He led them to the tombs, a place represented by death and where dangerous, out-of-control people were condemned. It makes sense that evil was comfortable in this dark place of doom and destruction. Yet, Jesus expected His disciples follow Him there. Why would Jesus allow His followers to get close to danger?

I can recall more instances of being out of control than I care to admit, especially as a mom. We Harbins are a passionate bunch. When we're glad, mad, and sad, we're loud. Passion is acceptable; out-of-control is not. I know I've given neighbors some good fodder to discuss a time or two.

As a mom, I've often categorized my passionate exclamations. Yelling, raising my voice, and even hollering get their own defense. Of course, whatever exclamation I spew depends on my mood. When combined with the infraction my precious child has committed, I'm then able to appropriately categorize the passionate outburst. Ridiculous, right? Passionate exclamations and out-of-control mothering are not the same. When I'm face to face with Jesus, He reveals the out-of-control behavior. And He desires to rescue me from that potential danger.

The Light of the World came to rescue and save all who place their trust in Him. Jesus had an appointment for a rescue on the dark beach that day. *The Son of the Most High-God* [see Mark 5:7] was on assignment to restrain and restrict what oppressed and tormented this man. The disciples were not immune to the temptation of becoming out of control, so Jesus allows them to be spectators of this man's rescue. And it wasn't farfetched to believe they already knew someone, or would one day meet someone, with the same oppressive need.

On the beach, rescue and danger face off as evil has a face-to-face encounter with Jesus. Evil knows its opponent, so Legion resorts to begging. Jesus is fully aware of Legion's stronghold. Jesus doesn't see a crazy person, He sees a man in danger and desires to rescue him. Jesus is wildly passionate about rescuing each of us from Satan's clutches. We were made to be loved by God, not ruled by evil. God's love goes deeper and is stronger than Satan's strongholds.

The disciples are captivated by this potentially dangerous encounter. They're rivetted to the rescue plan unfolding before their eyes. It's so easy to get distracted by all that's going on. Gawking and gaping at an out-of-control crazy person has no lasting value or benefit. The disciples have a front row seat to this rescue mission. It's imperative they keep their attention more on the Rescuer than the rescue plan.

KEY POINT: GOD'S RESCUE MUST BE DONE GOD'S WAY

Mark 5:11-12 informs us "A large herd of pigs was feeding on the nearby hillside. The demons begged Jesus, 'Send us among the pigs; allow us to go into them." This isn't the first time evil has witnessed a rescue by the Most High God. Evil knows the power of Jesus; therefore, Legion attempts to manipulate Jesus with what appears to be a good idea. But Jesus isn't swayed by their directive because Jesus is Spirit-led and knows this rescue plan is not about transferring evil but about saving a life. Evil is no match for Jesus Christ!

If this man is to be rescued, it must be done God's

way. Legion is at home in this region, but Jesus is about to change their address. Evil is willing to leave the man but remain in the vicinity. Godly rescue is a holy rescue, wholly reclaiming and restoring. An address change will not do. Annihilation is God's rescue plan.

If you haven't heard about the herd, pay close attention. In Mark 5:13 it appears Jesus gives Legion what he asked for. But when Jesus gave permission for Legion to enter the pigs, it was a holy decision not a scheme for evil-preservation.

When the evil spirits had holy permission, they came out of the man and went into the herd of pigs. Over 582,000 pounds of pork became the destination for evil. For the breakfast lover, that's close to 300 pounds of bacon. But, this is not about the loss of a herd; it's about the rescue of a man. And this man is in a battle with evil. Fighting a strong enemy requires strong fighting power. The man was weary, weak, and worn-out, his strength depleted. Man is no match for the powers, principalities, and rulers of darkness. But Jesus is man's worthy warrior.

The rescue plan involves preservation, but first, an extermination is called for. Though the evil spirits begged to be sent into the pigs, ultimate authority belonged to Jesus. He had the final word. Legion has no recourse when Jesus is on the scene. His permission was required, so Jesus granted Legion a leave of absence from the man. Legion had expectations – make the herd his home. But Jesus doesn't fight this battle Legion's way.

Mark 5:13 continues, "...The herd...rushed down the steep bank into the lake and were drowned." See? Legion does remain in the region, but God declared their doom.

Earlier this same night, the disciples witnessed Jesus rebuke the winds and the waves. And with the same authority, they've now heard Him call evil out of an out-of-control man and into a herd of pigs. Followers of Jesus are witnesses to His mighty acts of rescue. And we shouldn't be silent about what we've seen.

KEY POINT: SHOW AND TELL

As Jesus shows His power, we're privileged to tell others about it. But, do we? What about the storms that internally rage? Jesus calms them. He also rescues us from evil. He restores, renews, and redeems our brokenness. Therefore, as His followers, it's our responsibility and it should also be our resolve to tell of what He's done.

Mark 5:14 says, "Those tending the pigs ran off and reported this and the people came to see what had happened." The pig farmers were bystanders. They weren't following Jesus. They were doing their job. Their report would have focused on what had happened to the pigs. Pieces of the account would be missing. To these people, the crazy and disoriented, the castoffs, unwanted and rejected ones belonged in this region. And now they're hearing about a crazed, demon-possessed individual, a lost herd of pigs, and a powerful man named Jesus. They can't help it...they're drawn to the other side.

The missing pieces are filled in as they arrive on scene. Mark 5:15 says, "When they came to Jesus, they saw the man who had been possessed by the legion of demons..." I love that they came to Jesus. God's Spirit wooed them to this spot. When Jesus has our attention, He can get us in a face-to-face encounter. The weary, weak, and worn out need to see Jesus. And we need to show and tell what Jesus has done in our life. Many people are lost and distraught and in need of His strength. We should be compelled to tell what His strength can do.

Here in Mark 5:15, the demon-possessed man is a

living testimony, the object of show and tell. Only, he's not on display. The mighty work of an all-powerful God is revealed through him. This castoff silently exhibits the change that occurs when Jesus rescues someone from evil's grip. Jesus has their attention, and the man bears the evidence of His work.

"...they saw the man...sitting there, dressed, and in his right mind..." The man was at the feet of Jesus. When was the last time anyone witnessed this out-of-control man quietly and calmly sitting? The verbiage denotes he seated himself. For any out-of-control man, that's a mighty act on its own. When Jesus rescues, the internal storms that rage and wreak havoc are calmed as well.

When Jesus has us in a face-to-face encounter, it's like His hands cup our face, open the eyes of our hearts, and spiritually gain our attention. Then others take notice of the emotional and physical changes. The people saw he was dressed, implying he was previously naked. Evil had this man exposed in all ways. Jesus completely covers him.

In Proverbs 31 we learn of a noble woman or the virtuous woman. The original word means strong, capable, and efficient – a warrior. She's loyal, hard-working, strong-willed, mighty, a force, and an army of one. Proverbs 31:25 says, "She's clothed with strength..." When we live as God intends, we're equipped and covered with His strength.

In Colossians 3:12-13, Paul exhorts followers of Jesus, who have set their hearts and minds to holy living, to be clothed in Christ's character. Compassion, kindness, humility, gentleness, patience, forbearance, and forgiveness make up the complete ensemble. And like an overcoat, love covers the entire outfit. Through Christ, we have all the covering we need.

When Adam and Eve ate what humanity was never meant to taste, sin entered their paradise, they realized they were naked, they hid from God, and they covered themselves with fig leaves they had sewn together. Man-made covering gets worn out, it weakens – it isn't a long-lasting outfit. It eventually fails. When God confronted Adam and Eve in their hiding place, He provided a more suitable covering.

In Genesis 3:21, it says, "The Lord God made garments of skin for Adam and his wife and clothed them." Through sacrifice, God provides the covering humanity needs. Immediately following the first committed sin, God demonstrated His deep love and amazing grace for Adam and Eve. He provided what they needed. Death was required for God to cover their nakedness.

God's covering plan brought His Son to earth where He allowed the sacrifice of Jesus, so we could be set free from the penalty and power of evil. We're not freed from the presence of evil until our physical body dies. God's greatest demonstration of show and tell is summed up in John 3:16 – "For God so loved the world that He gave His one and only son..." and Romans 5:8 – "But God demonstrates his own love for us in this: while we were still sinners, Christ died for us." When God shows up in our life, we get to tell all about it.

Mark 5:15 tells us not only is the once out-of-control man dressed and calmly sitting, he's also "...in his right mind..." The Greek language says he's *sophreneo*. Phonetically it's *so-fron-eh`o*. This verb means he's actively in his right mind and exercising self-control. This man had a presence of distinct soundness of thought.

KEY POINT: SOPHRON IS SPOT ON

Self-control and self-discipline allow us to think and act properly. When Jesus ordered the evil out, it was like the sun dawned where a dark cloud hovered. As you're traveling on a highway, perhaps you've experienced darkness rolling in as a storm develops ahead. Sunglasses are shed and headlights turned on as heightened senses are alerted. Sophreneo is activated. Once the storm ceases, calm and peace reign – in and out of the vehicle.

The strength Jesus enabled internally shows up externally as demonstrated in the man sitting dressed and in his right mind. The end of Romans 12:2 says, "...be transformed by the renewing of your mind..." When Jesus takes over the out-of-control areas, your mind is renewed – it's been renovated, displaying a complete change for the better.

Paul wrote a letter to a man named Titus encouraging him to teach about a faith lived out well. In Titus 1:5, Paul writes, "...that you might straighten out what was left unfinished..." Yes, Jesus turns us from evil and desires we live as He intends. At times, we need to be straightened out. Titus 2:3-5 does this for women.

Paul says the older women – that's spiritually, not physically older – should be taught to be reverent in the way they live. In other words, if you've followed Jesus for some time now, it should be evident. He goes on to say they shouldn't be slanderers or calumniators, people who make false and malicious statements against another.

I've been on the receiving end of a calumniator. It's hard and it hurts – especially when the Christian slinging the slander is a close friend. Our friendship suffered – it broke up because of her refusal to handle the situation with truth and grace. However, through the difficult calumny, God straightened me out. He revealed a witness for Jesus is paused when a false testimony is spread. And that has lasting effects far greater than any hurt I'll ever experience.

Paul's letter to Titus has more to say to the mature follower. She shouldn't be addicted to much wine but to teach what is good. It doesn't say *and* teach what is good; it says *but*. That infers the latter is the better option. Before you expel a heavy breath, eyeroll, or ever-so-slightly shake your head, I am not going to make the blanket statement *Christians should not drink alcohol*. Yes, I have opinions and thoughts, but first, let's look at two words in Titus 2:5, "...be self-controlled..."

Be sophron. Sophron is the adjective to the verb, sophreneo. When mature followers of Jesus observe Paul's counsel to Titus, they're able to set an example for the new believer, the recent convert, the undeveloped disciple. Two words translate many ways.

- Be wise
- Be sober-minded
- Be sensible
- Be self-controlled
- Be discreet
- Be temperate
- Be virtuous
- Be sober

According to dictionary.com, sober means sedate in demeanor, habitually temperate, and showing self-control as well as refraining from drink. The Greek word has multiple meanings, too – a sound mind, sane, in one's senses, self-controlled, temperate, and curbing one's desires and impulses.

A woman who curbs is controlled, restrained, and in-check. Consider what happened when an uncontrolled desire or out-of-control impulse influenced a certain decision in your life. Curbs near the street have function, separating the road from the roadside and discouraging parking or driving on sidewalks and lawns. Curbs can also be used for structural support and to channel runoff water into the storm drain.

Likewise, curbing desires and impulses keeps a follower of Jesus from going where she doesn't belong, supports her ability to have self-control, and helps manage the debris from the storms that rage.

The year was 1995. Kevin and I were out to dinner celebrating our seventh anniversary in a beautiful, quaint, popular restaurant in Lexington, KY. Kevin was halfway through seminary. We were poor. An evening out, especially at this establishment, was rare. We left the four children (all under the age of six) with a babysitter. I didn't have to wipe any faces, cut anyone's food, take anyone to the restroom, stop any bickering, calm any fidgeting – it was a glorious evening.

On the way to the restaurant we reminisced about our honeymoon – how we walked into that coastal restaurant in Maine just before closing time. They served us anyway. We had extra-special treatment. Our water glasses were constantly filled, the bread was fresh, our food delicious. And the bottle of wine, satisfying. We kept the empty bottle as a souvenir.

The memory influenced us to order a carafe of the same alcoholic beverage. After the waiter poured the red Bordeaux into the stemmed glassware, Kevin made our toast, we clinked the glasses, and took the celebratory sip. It tasted good. Our meal was served, and conversation continued. We spoke of dreams and goals. We envisioned Kevin's first appointment, the church he'd be assigned to by the governing body within our denomination.

I don't recall how far into the carafe we were, but I

succinctly remember the question quietly posed by Kevin. "Why are we doing this? Why are we drinking?" We set the stemware down. I can't recall our exact dialog, but I remember the outcome.

We considered the couple at a nearby table and pretended they were from our future church, making Kevin their pastor. We concocted a story pretending the man struggled with alcohol. Would it impact them seeing their spiritual leader consume what was out-of-control in his life?

I know what some of you are thinking – *it's none of their business what you do in your free time* or *it was a carafe, not a keg* or *that's your story, not mine.* The retorts are many. You're right, this is my story, but God's Word is for all Christians. And He says to be sophron.

Omniscience is spot on. The moment we come into relationship with an all-knowing God, we became his witnesses – bearing His character, wearing His name – a living testimony of His amazing grace. Since it's God's directive to *be sophron*, I became aware it was Him calling me to step away from alcohol. I had a decision to make. God's commands are not suggestions; therefore, it's no longer about my opinion, rather, it's a matter of obedience.

I desire and choose to live as Jesus intends. I don't want to malign the testimony I live out for Jesus. Sophron implies I must be of sound mind. (And, yet, one glass of wine affects the mind.) Sophron entails curbing my desires. (Yes, the sight and smell of the fruity drink is tempting.)

What Paul wrote to Christians in Titus is for all of us today. For the followers of Jesus who post details to Facebook and pictures to Instagram declaring wine as their common go-to for rest, revival, and restoration, Paul says,

"...be sophron..."

After Paul writes to Titus about the spiritually older folks teaching the spiritually younger ones to be sophron, he adds to teach them to be pure – immaculate, clean, chaste, and modest – from every fault. In the 1800's, Ivory soap was sent to college chemistry professors and independent laboratories for a purity analysis. The ingredients that didn't fall into the category of pure equaled 56/100%. The famous soap is still known as 99.4% pure.

One Sunday morning, at a former church my husband pastored, in-between songs, the leader attempted to encourage the congregation by saying, "God can handle 95% of the problems represented here today." After the singing concluded, Pastor Kevin stood, and said, "I need to correct what was just said. God can handle 100% of the issues represented here today. We can't have anyone thinking their issue is included in the 5%."

Pure is pure, nothing is mixed in. Impurity of the .06% is a miniscule amount, but it's still impure. In the letter to Titus, Paul says to teach the spiritually young women to be pure after he says to teach them to be sophron.

I wouldn't accept 99.4% devotion from my husband. And he wouldn't want that from me. Our oneness, our marriage and needs and require us to be fully and completely and purely devoted to one another – nothing should get mixed in to the relationship. Sophron is spot on when followers of Jesus live purely, with nothing mixed in or competing for their relationship with Jesus.

For the man calmly sitting, dressed, and in his right mind in Mark 5:15, I wonder how he would feel if Jesus ordered 99.4% of the evil into the pigs? That would leave .06% of evil still taking up residence in his heart and mind. Would he be ok with that? Would that amount of evil be tamped down and hushed up, never to oppress the man again?

Jesus hung on the old rugged cross and died for all our sin. As the old song declares, He's got the whole world in His hands – He doesn't exclude .06%. His love, His care, His grace, His forgiveness is spot-on.

KEY POINT: WE SHOULD BE AWESTRUCK AT JESUS

Mark 5:15 records the response to those who came to Jesus, "...and *they* were afraid." [emphasis mine] If we read this in the context of our English language, we'd think they were in fear of the man. But that's not the case. The Greek word for afraid is *phobeo*, which looks and sounds like phobia, a persistent and irrational fear. Though the Greek definition is similar, there's another meaning – reverence. According to dictionary.com, revere is to regard with respect tinged with awe.

They were in awe of what Jesus has done. *They* reverently regarded the obvious change they saw in the man. They knew this man. They've heard his outbursts and witnessed his out-of-control behaviors. They were astonished at the power of Christ displayed through this man's calm demeanor. Previously, they were afraid of the man. Now they're in awe of the Son of Man.

When Jesus shows up and shows off in our life, that's news we should spread to give others something to be awestruck about. People love to spread news about other people. Let's give them the outrageous, far-fetched, and out-of-this-world reports of Jesus turning around the out-of-control conduct in our lives. The wonder-working power of Jesus exploding in our lives should have us all awestruck.

KEY POINT: WE'RE STRENGTHENED BY TELLING OTHERS ABOUT JESUS

In Mark 5:18, Jesus is getting back in the boat and the man follows, begging to go with Jesus. Can you blame him? For the first time in ages, the man feels safe and has a renewed purpose. His face-to-face encounter connected him to Jesus. He thinks being in the boat with Jesus will allow him the strength he needs to live his transformed life.

But Jesus says no. Is He heartless? Of course not! Is He done with the man? No way! Is the boat crowded? That's not the point.

When Jesus renovates a life, when a true transformation takes place and He turns evil around, persons want to be as close to Him as possible. Some avoid their family and friends. Others spend more time inside the church building serving and doing and helping than they do in their neighborhoods. Yes, Christians are stronger when they're together. But what about the people you know and love? If not you, then who? Who will show and tell the people in your life – *your* family, *your* friends, *your* neighbors, *your* co-workers – what Jesus has done for you?

It's true – being surrounded by Christians, spending more time at church serving in all the capacities, and, yes, absolutely being in the boat with Jesus gives us strength. But so does being a witness for Jesus and sharing what He's done for us.

Though Jesus wouldn't let him in the boat, He still had another plan to strengthen this man on his faith journey. "Go home to your family and tell them how much the Lord has done for you and how he has had mercy on you." (Mark 5:19)

Strength comes from obedience. Imagine if the man would have walked away in the opposite direction of home. We know the evil that left would not have run up the embankment and back into his life. However, consequences from not doing as Jesus said would be his new reality. This man chose well.

Mark 5:20 reports, "So the man went away and began to tell...how much Jesus had done for him. And all the people were amazed." The King James Version says it this way, "...and all men did marvel." People were astonished and filled with wonder at the extraordinary things Jesus had done.

The out-of-control are weary, weak, worn out and need a face-to-face encounter with Jesus. Others marvel at His wonder-working power, and we stand strong as we tell them all the marvelous things Jesus does.

PONDER

deeply, carefully, and thoughtfully consider

1. What does out-of-control look like for you?

2. EVIL spelled backward is LIVE.

    a. What backward thing (anything contrary to God's Word) has you weary, weak, or worn out?

    b. How has Jesus tried to rescue you from this backward thing and you've ignored, avoided, or doubted it?

3. Lasting strength comes from God.

    a. How can you gain more of His strength to lessen or deplete the out-of-control moments?

b. Consider coming up with a *personal control plan* to live by. What does this look like for you?

PERSUADE

God's Word influences, encourages, and guides

1. Read Proverbs 25:28. How does this verse guide you to a better understanding of the dangers of being out of control.

2. Find 2 Peter 1:3-8 and respond to the following:

   a. (vs. 3) What does God's power give us?

   b. (vs. 4) How is God's Word described?

   c. (vs. 4) How do followers of Jesus escape worldly corruption?

d. (vs. 5-7) Name the faith additives:

_____   _____

_____   _____

_____   _____

_____

e. (vs. 8) What's the benefit of these qualities growing inside a Christian?

PRACTICAL

applying Biblical Truth to present day

1. Look back on the KEY POINTS in chapter three. Which one can help you to stand strong when living out-of-control? Why?

1. Show and Tell isn't just for Elementary students. And it isn't only for the man in Mark Chapter 5. Go to an unsaved friend, or a wayward follower of Jesus, and show them His wonder-working power in your life and tell them how it encourages, uplifts, and makes you strong.

2. Titus 2:5 tells followers to be self-controlled.

   a. What's the Greek word?

   b. How does curbing desires and impulses help you to stand strong?

PERSONAL

inviting Jesus into your current reality

1. On a scale of 5 to 1, with 5 being enraged and 1 being calm, rate your level of out-of-control in the areas below. Invite Jesus to show up and show off in the areas of concern.

Rushed Mornings _____

Frantic Dinner Prep _____

Difficult Co-workers _____

Testy Neighbors _____

Belligerent Child _____

Angry with Spouse _____

Sunday morning and late to church _____

Unmet Expectations _____

Financial Burden _____

Flat Tire _____

Restaurant Messes up Your Order _____

Friend Stands You Up _____

2. Galatians 5:22-23 names the Fruit of the Spirit. Nine parts make up one fruit. Starting with the one that naturally comes easy and ending with the one you're most challenged with, list them here.

a.

b.

c.

d.

e.

f.

g.

h.

i.

j.

This fruit evidences Jesus lives in you, apply it to your daily life.

4
strength for the CALLOUSED

"Be strong in the Lord and in his mighty power."
Ephesians 6:10

I have never had a pedicure. Many have told me I'm nuts. Not one convincing argument has caused me to change my mind. As a strong-willed woman, that's a challenge. Attempting to sway a strong will only makes the strong will stronger. It's the way of a stubborn one. Try and move the immoveable, and their will only sets deeper.

My husband loves to have his feet massaged. You see, my aversion to pedicures isn't a strong-will issue. I don't like feet. I don't want to touch any foot, and I don't want anyone touching my foot. I can't even scratch the bottom of my own foot. The thought alone gives me the heebie-jeebies. Yes, this causes a dilemma in our marriage as Kevin Harbin is married to a foot hater. But covenant love must sacrifice. If he puts a clean sock on, I'll massage my man's feet. Oh, the sacrifices we make for one another.

Feet tend to be calloused. Thickened areas of the skin form from repeated friction or pressure. When my son was in high school, he didn't like that he had small feet, so he wore his basketball shoes a size larger. (Don't try and make sense of it. As I said, he was a teenager.) The carelessness gave his feet extra room to slip and slide causing giant, disgusting calluses. His stubborn decision had consequences.

KEY POINT: CALLOUS IS A CONSEQUENCE
Notice the last phrase of Mark 6:52 says, "...their

hearts were hardened." Disciples of Jesus were hard hearted. Followers of Jesus resisted God's ways. Today, they'd be considered close-minded Christians, dull devotees. As I read and study this phrase, varying emotions fluctuate in my head and heart. My stubborn side leans toward snide and snarky. *Stupid disciples, my word. They're face-to-face with Jesus every single day and their hearts are hard? You've got to be kidding me! Close-minded and dull; they can't even see what's right in front of their noses. Open your eyes, guys! He fed 5000 people with a boy's Happy Meal – you witnessed it! And you were in the boat when Peter walked on water. Wake up! You've got it so much easier than we do today.*

But then there's the empathetic side leaning towards appreciation and affinity. A personal acknowledgement and understanding of their plight has me thinking *Man, I've been there. I get it, disciples, following Jesus isn't easy. We fall, we fail, we get our eyes off Him and start doubting and questioning His ways and His wonders. It's tough, I know. I can't imagine what it was like to watch those loaves and fish increase to feed the multitudes. And then there's Peter – what was he thinking getting out of the boat in the middle of the sea?*

See how I can be towards the disciples? Calloused, yet empathic. Hardened, yet compassionate.

Conflict, pressure, and friction form calluses on the heart of a follower of Jesus. Christians know conflict. People cause pressure. Followers understand friction. When we avoid, mishandle, or ignore the conflict, pressures, and friction, we experience consequences.

A calloused heart brings consequence, but the callous has a starting point. We intentionally began at the end of this story in Mark Chapter 6. But every story has a starting point, so let's back up and look at Mark 6:45.

"Immediately, Jesus made His disciples get into the boat and go on ahead of Him...while He dismissed the crowd."

KEY POINT: NOT ALL STARTING POINTS ARE OBVIOUS

In my Bible just above Mark 6:45 is the caption *Jesus Walks on Water*. The subheading tells us what to expect in the next section. When we see separations in Scripture, whether by chapter, verse, or how they're sectioned out, we need to be careful when making assumptions. Separation helps bring order and understanding to where to find certain stories and narratives. On our quest to find where the callous begins, we can't assume it was in Mark 6:45 just because of the separation between accounts.

Before we read about their hard hearts, we're told where the callous began. In Mark 6:52 it says, "For they had not understood about the loaves..." Other versions say it like this:

- It wasn't clear to them about the bread [The Bible in Basic English]
- They considered not the miracle of the loaves [King James version]
- They had not gained any insight from the incident of the loaves [New American Standard Bible]
- They didn't understand the significance of the miracle [New Living Translation]
- They hadn't learned the lesson taught by the loaves [Weymouth New Testament]

They hadn't caught what Jesus taught. That's not the issue. They had a great deal of catching to do as Jesus was constantly teaching, preaching, and performing miracles. Every day was filled with lessons galore. Some would slip by unnoticed. What one disciple caught, another might miss. You see, Jesus didn't come to only educate His disciples. He came to earth to reveal God's plan of redemption, restoration, and revival.

My dad reminds me often that studying and reading the Bible is all about revelation, not education. When disciples only look to be educated, they'll miss things. But when disciples have their eyes completely fixed and focused on Jesus, what gets taught will then be caught.

A calloused heart conceals what God reveals. When followers of Jesus avoid, mishandle, or ignore God's Word, callouses form. It wasn't that the disciples didn't get it; it was that they took their eyes off Jesus, stopped talking about what they had witnessed, and pushed it out of their minds. As the saying goes, out of sight, out of mind.

Mark 6:45 informs us Jesus made them get into a boat while He stayed behind. Perhaps the disciples were so focused on what was next because not only did they push aside the previous miracle, but no one thought to ask Jesus how he was going to meet up with them across the lake since they took the boat and He remained on shore.

These disciples loved Jesus. They gave up everything to follow Him. They were committed to remaining by His side. But when followers have their eyes off Jesus, even for just a moment, the slip has us slide to places we never planned and are hard to imagine. When Jesus stayed on the shore and their boat slipped into the water, they weren't thinking *He'll just walk out to us when he's done.* No way had they considered that!

As obedient followers, Jesus said get in the boat, and they did. But they're also ignorant followers. Ignorant is not stupid; it's uninformed. They were willing to trust Jesus with their next step; however, they ignored where their feet had just been. And that's the starting point of their calloused hearts.

KEY POINT: WE BENEFIT FROM BOTH WINDSHIELDS AND REARVIEW MIRRORS

I use this vehicle analogy often. Each vantage point offers vision: forethought and foresight. The windshield shows us a panoramic view of where we're headed. As the disciples got into the boat, they had foresight. They knew where they were headed, and they looked out in the direction the vessel would take them.

The rearview mirror has benefit, too. It allows the driver a snapshot of what's behind. I hadn't been driving long when I hit a bird. It couldn't be avoided. I had two options: swerve into traffic or send the feathers flying. A glance in the rearview mirror showed floating feathers, proving the better choice was made.

My friend was recently involved in an auto accident. The view out her windshield showed the traffic was starting to slow. As she prepared in advance to brake, a natural glimpse in her rearview mirror unsettled her. Horror replaced caution as the vehicle behind her wasn't using the panoramic view to his advantage. In a split second, my friend was rear-ended at a high rate of speed.

If you saw the pictures of the back of her SUV, you'd wonder if serious injury occurred. My friend's face looked like she was a prize fighter, but she stands strong to tell of God's protection. The rearview gave her forethought of what was to come.

On our spiritual trek, we benefit by looking back. Snapshots through the rearview teach us lessons as we walk by faith. The disciples had foresight as they looked ahead, but they disregarded forethought. Oblivious, callouses formed on their hearts.

Mark 6:47-48a goes on to say, "When evening came, the boat was in the middle of the lake, and [Jesus] was alone on land. He saw the disciples straining at the oars, because the wind was against them..."

KEY POINT: AS WE STRAIN, WE MUST REMAIN FIRM IN OUR FAITH

It's no secret life is hard. But your heart doesn't need to follow suit. In the middle of glad, sad shows up. In the middle of calm, the wind blows. In the middle of joy, tragedy interrupts. It's the way of life. A piece of literature discloses *the best laid plans*. No matter how careful we plan, something can still go wrong. For followers of Jesus, this is the question: when the winds of strife are against us, will we look for a snapshot to help us in our current reality? Will we glance at the rearview mirror as we strain at the oars in the middle of the unplanned and unforeseen chaos?

The disciples rowed away from shore and left Jesus on the beach. Yes, He planned it that way. But just because He isn't in the boat doesn't mean His presence shouldn't be known or noticed. The account doesn't say the disciples looked back toward the beach to get a glimpse of the one they left standing there. It doesn't say they sent out a distress signal. They're sailors; surely, they could send an S.O.S.

A lot of people think the international distress signal is an abbreviation for *save our souls* or *save our ship*, and though that's not factual, it is applicable to the disciples here in Mark Chapter six. As they grip the oars attempting to right the boat, they must decide how they'll handle the wind. Though it rages, it doesn't have to control them. According to Isaiah 25:4, God is a refuge for the distressed and a shelter from the storm.

We won't find where God promises a storm-free existence, but we will read many promises of His presence in the storm. Through the torrents, we lose focus and the winds divert our attention.

KEY POINT: AS WE LOOK AT THE STORM, JESUS LOOKS OUT FOR US

Notice this book's cover design. To me, mountains are a sign of strength. They're sturdy, solid, stable, and secure. No wind can blow a mountain over nor shift it off its foundation. When my computer is in screensaver mode, the side of a mountain fills the screen. One man measures approximately half-an-inch tall as he stands on the mountainside. As he clings to the rock, I'm reminded where I must stand. Isaiah 26:4 (The Amplified version) says, "Trust in the Lord forever. For the Lord God is an everlasting Rock [the Rock of Ages]."

I have many memories of summer vacations as a child. For years, our family rented a cabin on the same large lake in the middle of Michigan. One beautiful day, my dad took my older sister, Susan, and me out on the rowboat. There were three metal benches in the boat. Dad took the middle to man the oars. Susan and I sat side-by-side in the back. I remember waving to mom who was on the shore, holding our little sister's hand. We were excited about our mini excursion.

Excitement ended when the wind blew, and clouds quickly formed. That's not unusual on an inland lake. Meteorologists can give the reason; I'll just tell my story. Summarizing, one loving and passionate dad fought wind and wave for his two terrified daughters. Dad had one of us move to the front of the boat to displace our weight for better balance. The clouds opened, and a hard, torrential downpour pelted our heads, shoulders, and backs. Dad rowed with all his might into the wind – getting his girls to safety was his goal.

For every strain at the oars, it seemed the wind deviated our course. Dad never gave in to the wind. Dad never allowed the waves to break his will. When rowing wasn't getting us to shore, he decided to move the boat parallel to land and in the direction of our destination. My sister and I were focused on the storm; dad was focused on rescue and safety. Not many are willing to jump out of a boat in the middle of a lake as the winds toss their tiny vessel about –unless passion and love are the motivator.

This story from Mark Chapter six is also found in Matthew 14:22-33. Each gospel shares exclusive aspects of the same story. If you and I witnessed the same event, we'd see different things; therefore, our retelling would have unique features. Mark mentions the wind. In Matthew 14:24, he references the boat being buffeted by the waves. Both accounts agree Jesus walked on water and when the disciples saw this, they were terrified, cried out in fear, and claimed He was a ghost.

Jesus loves His disciples so much He can't take His eyes off them. In the middle of their current chaos, and out of His everlasting love, Jesus initiates a face-to-face encounter. They're terrified and hallucinating, yet Jesus gets their attention.

Matthew 14:27 and Mark 6:50 record the same words, "Take courage! It is I. Don't be afraid." Notice the progression. In three small sentences, with one breath, and a familiar voice, Jesus rebukes, reminds, and reprimands.

We like sheep have gone astray (Isaiah 53:6). The sheep listen to His voice...Jesus is the Good Shepherd

(John 10:2, 14). When sheep get off course, it's the shepherd's voice that guides them back.

The disciples are like lost sheep. The wind and waves caught them off guard. With their attention on the storm, they can't recognize Jesus standing on the water. As their Good Shepherd, He knows they know His voice, so before getting in the boat, Jesus speaks. But not all His words are feel-good words. When followers avoid, mishandle, or ignore God, corrective and authoritative verbiage is required.

"Susan! Ellen! Listen to me!" Dad said with authority, getting our attention back on him. "I'm getting out of the boat and walking us to safety." We didn't argue or offer a different plan. He was dad and he called the shots. We trusted his words. As dad readied himself to climb out of the boat, it lurched, and he straddled the side. I remember seeing agony and pain on his face, but remember, passion and love kept him motivated. Dad had more success walking us to safety than he did at the oars. As the storm subsided, we arrived safely home. My dad was my hero that day. Years later, I learned of the surgery required to repair the injury he sustained when he straddled the boat that day.

I have snapshots in my rearview mirror of a love that wouldn't give up. I see a father steadily trudging through stormy waters to get his girls to safety. I caught the courage my dad displayed to stand strong as a storm wreaked havoc.

KEY POINT: FOLLOW WITH GUTS, BUT DON'T IGNORE THE GUST

Matthew 14:28 adds detail and dialogue not found in Mark's account. "Lord, if it's you,' Peter replied, "tell me to come to you on the water." Impulsive, yet gutsy, Peter responds to Jesus. Peter is ready to jump ship. In this moment, Peter is all in.

Impulsivity is a good thing, yet it can be an impediment. It can be daring, yet, stupid; fun, yet woeful. What seems like a great idea in the moment can quickly turn.

Let's look closely at Peter's gutsy move. He went from thinking Jesus was a ghost to being willing to jump out of the boat with a faith that can move mountains – or walk on water, whatever the case may be. Impulsivity has no room for forethought. Some Type-A personality types are incapable of putting themselves in the place of Peter. If this is you, you're not broken. As one man jumps out of the boat, eleven others stay put. The wind and waves have nothing on their crazy and gutsy friend. Remaining doesn't make them any less a disciple.

Just because Peter was the one to jump at the chance to walk on water doesn't mean the others aren't walking by faith. Seated or jumping in the boat or walking on water – each follower will benefit from Peter's face-to-face encounter with Jesus.

Not all are called out of the boat, but all are called to take courage. Yes, Peter had the guts to jump, but Jesus spoke to all the disciples when he said, "Take courage!" Though Peter's courage took him out of the boat, the others took hold from their seats.

As they took Jesus at his Word, the storm continued to churn the water and the waves tossed the vessel. Taking courage didn't stop the gusts of wind. Yet, Jesus remained with His courageous followers. Peter's gutsy charge of *Lord, if it's you,* involves a powerful and doubt-filled word. There is no *if* about it. Jesus – who, incidentally, hours earlier, fed over 5000 people with five loaves and two fish, with plenty of leftovers – walks on water!

If the disciples were looking in the rearview for the snapshots of that great feast, their faith would be increased in this moment of fear. Before gutsy, impulsive Peter jumped, he wondered *if* the man walking on water was Jesus.

Only Jesus could walk on water, but we've not seen that before. We saw him calm the sea a while back, that's not new, but here is a man walking on water before my very eyes. It must be Jesus, I want out of this boat, now!

Peter stood up and said, "...tell me to come to you on the water." Don't mistake this as a disciple telling Jesus what to do. Jesus wouldn't have spoken the next word if Peter's request was out of God's will.

"Come," Jesus said. And with that one word, Peter steps out of the boat and onto a platform of water. The winds and waves continued their ferocious assault on the boat, but Peter stood strong on the tumultuous water. You can be assured snapshots of this moment were being taken, and hopefully, stored in every disciple's memory bank.

Peter walked toward Jesus. Granted, his feet are on water, but all the disciples were challenged in this moment to move toward Jesus. Consider this: Can a Christian get closer to Jesus if she stands still on her faith journey? A closer walk with Jesus requires we step toward Jesus. Otherwise, we dwell in mediocrity or ride the proverbial fence. Sitting atop a spiritual fence is like my dad who straddled the boat – it comes with consequence and pain.

In Revelation 3:15-16, Jesus has something to say to fence riders and those who dwell in mediocrity, or as Jesus says, followers who are neither hot nor cold. Lukewarm disciples better decide which side of the fence they're on.

15"I know your deeds, that you are neither cold nor hot. I wish you were either one or the other! 16 So, because you are lukewarm – neither hot nor cold – I am about to spit you out of my mouth."

We're all familiar with followers who are on fire for Jesus – their flame is stoked, ready to move mountains or cheer you on from the boat as you walk on water. We've also met the one who at one time burned bright but allowed their flame to flicker, then falter, and finally, fail. A digression of light, and a refusal to fan the flame, threatens that faith journey.

Jesus would rather we step toward Him and keep in step with Him. For the on-fire, burning-bright believers, their feet are pointed toward Jesus. They're in a face-to-face encounter with Jesus, their eyes fixed and focused on Him as they walk by faith. The winds gust, but they have their eyes locked on their Savior. Whether they jump out or remain in the boat, they fully trust Jesus.

A cold Christian is one who gets carried away by the wind and waves. A strong gust determines her stance and they became cold – a distant follower no longer desiring to walk by faith or to live as Jesus intends. If you've fallen on the cold side of the fence, Jesus welcomes you back with open arms. You may have stopped pursuing Him, but He never stops wooing you back to His embrace.

However, the one who sits on the fence between the fanned flame and the burnt-out wick makes God sick. Literally, that one is the vomit of God. I can remember the day well when the realtor showed up on our doorstep ready to show his clients our recently-on-the-market house. We had just committed to walk by faith and follow God as He called Kevin to seminary. It required he quit a successful career, we sell our home, move to another state, and trust God to provide for our needs.

We were burning bright for Jesus. Having a realtor wanting to show our house should have had me excited. And I was, except we had an agreement – I would need at least an hour to tidy the place and pack up the kids before strangers could tour our house. (That night, the realtor neglected to call.)

At that time, we had a three-year-old daughter and two-year-old and three-month-old boys. And they were all sick. "Mommy, my tummy feels funny," was the clue from my three-year-old before she threw up on the kitchen floor. Moments later, the two-year-old walked over to where I sat on the sofa and, well, how can I delicately, yet dramatically convey, his diaper couldn't hold the explosive contents. As I considered how to take care of both dilemmas, the baby puked all over me. Not baby spit-up, but rather a projectile eruption that shocked me how it could come out of such a tiny human.

As I'm covered in vomit and the stench of diaper contents hovered heavy in the air, the doorbell rang. I could have pretended not to be there, but that wouldn't have the same effect, now, would it? I answered the door, with the stench reaching them before my greeting. "I'm sorry, now isn't a good time," I said with a fake smile and a tone like Mrs. Cleaver from that 1960's sitcom portraying her and her home to be *just fine*.

I can't imagine anyone intentionally and consciously becoming the vomit of God. If you find yourself riding the fence, you better fall on one side or the other. Lukewarm is a litmus test for followers, revealing our true stance as a believer.

Peter was on fire for Jesus when he jumped up and stepped out of the boat. A hot follower stands strong when she wholeheartedly trusts Jesus. Peter was strong as he stepped toward Jesus until he glanced in a different direction. Matthew 14:30 says, "But when [Peter] saw the wind, he was afraid and [began] to sink..."

2 Corinthians 5:7 says, "We walk by faith, not by sight." Literally it means to regulate our life by faith. Our steps should be ordered by God, and His Word should dictate our faith journey. Following God's ways controls our stance.

Peter heard the howl of the wind and lost his guts as the gust got his attention. Instead of being in awe that he was walking on water, he stood in fear of the wind. For a split second, fear had Peter on the fence, leaning to the cold side. And he sank. Impulsivity had Peter wanting to jump out of the boat. Instinctively, a momentary fear had him crying out to Jesus for help, "Lord, save me!"

Jesus always lends a hand to followers who fall off the fence and land on the cold side if they earnestly call on Him for help. Matthew 14:31 records how Jesus responds to Peter's cry for help, "Immediately, Jesus reached out his hand and caught [Peter]. 'You of little faith,' [Jesus] said, 'why did you doubt?"

Jesus catches Peter, and Peter grabs tightly to Jesus as he's about to go under.

KEY POINT: A CALLOUSED HEART CAN TAKE US DOWN

Perhaps this is where the idiom *with a sinking heart* comes from. Jesus knows when our hearts are being carried away by the storms of life. He knows the condition of our heart before we avoid, mishandle, or ignore God's will or His way.

Proverbs 28:14 says, "Blessed is the man who always fears the Lord, but he who hardens his heart falls into trouble." When Peter was walking on water, he was dwelling in the fear of the Lord. As soon as he looked away from Jesus he fell into trouble. And that fall terrified Peter, because it has grave consequences. But sinking to the bottom of the sea isn't the most ominous.

A calloused heart is more serious and solemn. Ephesians 4:18 says, "They are darkened in their understanding and separated from the life of God because of the ignorance that is in them due to the hardening of their hearts." Going under, sinking beneath the weight of a heavy heart, is a dark existence.

Peter went from hot to cold in a heartbeat. His lack of faith needed a rebuke, and his doubt needed a reprimand. Some of you might think Jesus was too harsh and would prefer Him to pull Peter into an embrace, hold him a bit, and speak soothing words of comfort to his wounded heart.

But, Jesus isn't there to lick wounds. Peter's heart condition is at stake – a callous is forming, with the threat of spiritual cardiac arrest, which will drag Peter to agonizing depths of despair.

In Proverbs 28:14, the meaning of the original word for *hardens* is stubborn, stiff-necked, and obstinate. In Ephesians 4:18, the verbiage the King James Version uses for *due to the hardening of their hearts* is *because of the blindness of their heart*. Research shows this word *blindness* is like that of a covering over a callous. A calloused heart continues to get worse – it can go blind, leaving a follower with dulled perception and a mind that is blunted, meaning stubborn and obdurate. Dictionary.com says obdurate is unmoved by persuasion, pity, or tender feelings; stubborn, unyielding, and stubbornly resistant to moral influence; persistently impenitent – having no regret for committed sins.

Do you see why Jesus doesn't take time to lick Peter's wounds? Peter's focus is still turned toward the face of

Jesus, and his ears are tuned to His voice. But there are eleven other reasons why Jesus doesn't give Peter the now-now pity party as he begins to sink.

The remaining disciples were paying attention as Peter impulsively chose to jump ship and they witnessed him fall. When Jesus rescues a follower from the dark depths of despair, doubt, disappointment, distress, or defeat, He's mindful of other Christians who are paying attention. Mark 6:51 picks up the story as Peter and Jesus get back in the boat. "...He [Jesus] climbed into the boat with them and the wind died down..."

Jesus didn't calm the storm for Peter when he wanted to walk on water. Jesus had a lesson to teach all disciples: No matter the storm, His presence is enough. When the winds blow, the waves crash, and we feel like Jesus isn't there or aware of our struggle, we can look in the rearview and see this snapshot of Jesus walking on water, drawing near to His followers in their storm.

KEY POINT: BE FULLY AMAZIED AT WHAT JESUS CAN DO

Christians with calloused hearts need to remember what Jesus has done. Followers who fall need to see Him at work. Discouraged disciples need Jesus to meet them in their despair. Everyone needs to believe Jesus loves you right where you are, but He loves you too much to leave you there. Whether we have a panoramic view or a front row seat or a glimpse from the rearview, as we witness the wonder-working power of Jesus, we should always be awestruck and fully amazed at His power.

Mark 6:42-43 says, "They all ate and were satisfied and the disciples picked up twelve basketfuls of broken pieces of bread..."

- Twelve disciples were satisfied. If they were at a table, they'd push their chair back, rub their contented bellies, and declare, "I'm full."

- Twelve disciples had twelve baskets *full* left over, reminding them of God's provision, the miracle Jesus performed, and the satisfaction Jesus brought to their life

- Twelve disciples sat in a boat with full stomachs but dull minds and calloused hearts because they *had not understood about the loaves.* They hadn't fully caught the lesson Jesus taught regarding the loaves. They hadn't fully grasped how wide and how deep the love and care of God is. And they hadn't fully understood the magnitude of His wonder-working miraculous power.

Jesus could have gotten in the boat and miraculously steered the boat to shore. However, He knew their heart condition, so He loved them right where they were, and without saying a word, the wind died down. And, as Mark 5:21 says, "...they were completely amazed."

PONDER

deeply, carefully, and thoughtfully consider

1. What kinds of things cause a calloused heart in a follower of Jesus?

2. Using the vehicle analogy, how did your faith grow because a rear-view glance offered forethought.

3. Now consider the consequences from the times you depended only on what you could see, and disregarded lessons previously learned.

PERSUADE

God's Word influences, encourages, and guides

1. In Matthew 14:24-26, imagine yourself being the strong disciple in the boat.

   a. What do you do or say to encourage the others when the storm rages?

   b. How do you help calm their fear?

   c. How would you react to Jesus walking on water?

2. In Matthew 14:27 and Mark 6:50, the words of Jesus are recorded in three small phrases.

   Take _____!

   It _____ _____.

   Don't _____ _____.

a. Which of these statements is difficult for you to trust?

b. Why is it hard?

3. According to Proverbs 28:14 and Proverbs 28:18, how do we stand strong?

PRACTICAL

applying Biblical Truth to present day

1. A calloused heart cannot stand strong. Ephesians 6:10-17 supplies us with what we need to stand strong.

    a. How many times is *stand* used in this passage?

    b. (vs. 10) Where does strength come from?

    c. (vs. 11) What do we need to stand strong?

c. (vs. 14-17) Name the pieces of armor.

1. _____ of _____

2. _____ of _____

3. _____ of _____

4. _____ of _____

5. _____ of _____

6. _____ of the _____

2. How can this armor protect your heart from being calloused?

5
strength for the RESOLUTE

"Be strong and let us fight bravely for our people..."
2 Samuel 10:12

Words. I'd rather speak them than write them. However, through voice, keyboard, or on paper, I find the more I write, the more I have to say. But I am a bit annoyed that legitimate words get misconstrued and their definitions modified.

Bomb. Somewhere along the way, this word became a slang term. It can mean to greatly fail (*I bombed that test*) or refer to something extremely entertaining or high quality (*that party was the bomb*).

Dog. What once only meant an animal and man's best friend has turned into feet. *These dogs sure are tired.* Immature people use it to refer to someone's facial looks. *She's a real dog.* And now the spelling has been altered to refer to a friend. *Hey, Dawg, what up?*

Then, there's goat. It went from being a hollow-horned, four-legged, mountainous creature to an idiom use for when one is angered, annoyed, or frustrated. *He really gets my goat.* Recently, it's used with a cute emoji depicting the hollow-horned creature, only it now represents the acronym for *Greatest Of All Time*.

Hijacked words.

Under each chapter title of this book, I've intentionally chosen a Bible verse with the word *strong* in each. For this chapter, 2 Samuel 10:12 is the verse. It encourages and demands...*be strong*. The King James version says *be of good courage*. Strong is courageous. The

New International Version goes on to say, "...let us *fight bravely*..." Over the last few years, I've noticed a demoting and degrading of this word *brave*.

When I got my first tattoo, I was told it was a brave thing to do. Really? I paid a man to permanently ink my ankle with a sun, representing the Light of the World, with six multi-hued colors representing the birthstone of myself, Kevin, and our four older kids. Two years later, I paid another artist to ink the top of my foot where two shooting stars appear to be falling from the sun, their colors represent our youngest two children whom we adopted. Tattooing my appendage didn't take bravery. It took creativity, cash, and commitment. Pronouncing I'm brave to be inked misconstrues and modifies the word.

When my children reached the age and maturity that we could leave them home alone, they weren't brave; rather, they were growing up and earning the honor of trust. However, when my eight-year-old son intervened on behalf of a boy being mistreated, when another son stood on the high-dive for hours working up the courage to jump, when my eleven-year-old daughter chose to walk out of a room at a party because a movie was chosen she knew wouldn't gain our approval, or anytime our kids said no to intense peer pressure, they were acting brave. When my son fought for our freedoms as a United States Marine, to me, he's brave.

Acts of bravery are not taking first steps, tying shoes, cutting their own meat, making their beds, cleaning their room without being told. In the Harbin House, they're expectations.

It's not brave when a lady chooses to cut her long hair short or change the wall color in her living room or ditch the minivan for a convertible. She might be motivated, inspired, or daring, but referring to ordinary changes as brave lowers the quality, deprives the value, and degrades the definition.

KEY POINT: IT'S TIME TO TAKE BRAVE BACK

In 2 Samuel 10:12, at its origin, brave is a courageous endurance. Brave faces difficulty with determination, brave faces danger with valiance, and brave faces pain with superior strength. Brave prevails, brave presses on in urgency, brave is firmly set and secure.

In the recent past, a certain hashtag movement helped ignite, shed light, and cause certain individuals to step into the fight against sexual assault, sexual harassment, and sexual abuse. And they do it with courageous endurance. Any victim of a heinous act who stands up and speaks out shows bravery. A silent, anonymous victim who faces her anguish and pain also exhibits bravery with courageous endurance. Loud and overt or quiet and reserved stand side by side in the fight against and to speak out regarding all abuse. Together, they *fight bravely*.

It's no secret that I cherish my spiritual upbringing. Morals and values were instilled. That doesn't mean I always followed or lived within those expectations. I've floundered, and I've failed along the way. But when a solid and firm foundation is laid, the principles resurface. (see Proverbs 22:6)

When godly principles are laid early, a follower of Jesus has a decision to make – live them out or ignore them. Recognizing tradition is similar. We can ignore the old ways simply because they're old, or we can glean from their strengths.

Growing up, we attended a church where prayer was taught, modeled, and trusted for healing, restoration, and wholeness. My parents didn't leave praying only to the pastor or Sunday School teachers – they brought it home. We prayed at mealtime and bedtime. We prayed when we were sick or hurt. We praised God, we pleaded with God, and with hearts of gratitude, we thanked God. As a young girl, I remember standing outside a closed door and pressing my ear to the panels, as my dad privately (or so he thought) prayed every morning. I tuned in long enough to hear him present my name to his Holy audience.

Growing up, the Sunday evening worship had a deep and abiding impact on my understanding of prayer. When I was eight-years-old, our church built a new sanctuary. Until that point, we worshiped in what later became the Fellowship Hall – the gathering spot for socializing, special events, and performances. Whatever space was the sanctuary, the altar rails were prominently displayed, with an expectation they'd be used for the intended purpose. Prayer.

Every Sunday I was in attendance – let's say I missed two Sundays a year (makes for easier math) until I was eighteen-years-old, meant I attended approximately (18 X 50) 900 worship services. I cannot recall one Sunday evening when someone was not kneeling at an altar rail. Not one time!

Foundation was laid. I know brave prayers were being sent to the throne of grace. I know some relied on bravery to walk the aisle and admit their need. I know brave tears and courageous sobs were poured out of broken souls. I was there, so I know. I knelt; therefore, I know.

Some people prevailed through prayer – they prayed the same plea for years, trusting the One who heard their repetitive petitions. Being on your knees for days, weeks, even years, imploring the Lord with prevailing prayers, comes from a superior strength.

Brave prayers are prayed by brave people, regardless if they feel the part. Courageous endurance is not mustering up some form of I-think-I-can; rather, it's rooted in a trust and unwavering faith in the One who hears the cry of your heart. Bravery stands strong through prayer.

KEY POINT: BRAVE HEROES

We don't always like to think of role models as heroes. If someone endures positively through a similar intense struggle, I refer to him as a hero. When someone overcomes an adversity or takes a righteous stand against a Scriptural injustice, she becomes my hero. When a woman rejects gossip, when she confronts a wrong, when she chooses to do the right thing no matter what, when she refuses to align with the masses, when so-called friends abandon her for her holy stance, she is my hero.

You don't need their last name but allow me to introduce you to some of my heroes: Linda, Mary, Jeanne, Erin, Amy, Beth, Sue, Sarah, Elsie, Cindy, Lea Ann, Bonnie, Christine, Pam, Hope, Barb, Katelyn, Alena, Kim, Sarah. It's certainly not an exhaustive list nor is it about their heroic deeds – it's about the bravery, their courageous endurance, and their ability to live it well, through difficulty, danger, or pain.

Now, allow me to introduce you to one of my Biblical heroes. She's a weary woman, yet despair drove her to Jesus. She's a worn-out mom in a valiant effort to never give up fighting for her daughter. And in her weakness, she's resolute, determined to get on her knees at the feet of Jesus.

Though unnamed, portions of Mark 7:25-26 support the introduction of this hero of mine. "...as soon as she heard about [Jesus...this mom] came and fell at his feet...and begged Jesus..."

KEY POINT: LATER NEVER HAPPENS

Ask any of our six children what the Harbin Family motto is, and without hesitation each will voice, "Later never happens." Put your shoes away! I'll do it later. No, you won't, because *later never happens*. Our motto gets applied in many ways with some more significant than others. I'll think, *I really should spend some quiet time with Jesus*, but the laundry needs shifting, the dishes need washing, the vacuum needs to be run, groceries need to be purchased...so I'll do it later. Most likely not, since we've learned *later never happens*.

My hero, in Mark Chapter 7, didn't wait until later to do something about her need. Perhaps we share this motto. As we read her story, it's with bravery she put the slogan into action. But, before we see what drove this brave woman to the feet of Jesus, let's reveal some facts.

Fact #1 – she's heard things. (Mark 7:25) Perhaps she's heard about the herd Jesus sent scurrying down that embankment. Maybe she heard about Peter walking on water or how Jesus fed that multitude of 5000 with a boy's lunch. It's possible she heard about the woman who touched the fringe of His cloak and her nonstop bleeding stopped. I wonder if she heard about the paralytic and the hole in the roof, or Peter's mother-in-law, or the crazy guy in the synagogue. For sure, she's heard things. And something she's heard made her go into action and fall at His feet.

Fact #2 – she's Greek. (Mark 7:26) That means she's not a Jew but a Gentile. She is unfamiliar with God's covenantal promises; she's unaware of the prophecies regarding the Messiah. Godly principles are not her foundation. Her faith is based only on what she's heard, not in what she knows.

Fact #3 – she fell at His feet. (Mark 7:25) I'm curious what thoughts were battling for space in her head as she was on her way to Jesus. Those voices can be loud and demanding and negative. *What a stupid decision. You know you're wasting your time. Your situation is a lost cause. What makes you think He'll pay attention to you? Do you really think He will stop whatever He's doing and listen to your concern?* A voice of discouragement lands on her despair but doesn't dissuade her objective – she must courageously get to Jesus and bravely fall at His feet.

Fact #4 – she's alone. (Mark 7:25 & 30) Today, a lot of women won't use a public restroom unless they go with a friend. As soon as she heard about Jesus, she left her home. She didn't make the time to invite a friend on her quest to get to Jesus.

When my son was on active duty, he was stationed at Camp Lejeune. Not counting the few months he was deployed to Afghanistan, the North Carolina base was his home. After his first four years, he had his heart set on re-enlisting. Serious medical issues with his legs, necessitated a medical retirement.

Andrew's issue required three surgeries; two on his left leg, one on the right. I took my son's need to Jesus and fell at His feet. As soon as Andrew's surgery was scheduled, a plan was set in motion for me to go to North Carolina and care for his recovery needs.

I'm an extrovert – being around people is my jam.

(The use of another hijacked word intended.) I process out loud, I think out loud, I laugh out loud, I emote out loud, and I even plan out loud. I prefer groups of people – the larger, the better (that way, I can meet and greet more people in a small space of time.) Sitting in a restaurant alone, going to the theater alone, vacationing alone all have one thing in common – alone. And that's not my comfort zone. It surprised others, me included, when the plan to help Andrew was to go to the North Carolina base, alone.

I learned things about myself on that first of three solo road trips to North Carolina. Though I prefer being with people, after fourteen hours in my vehicle I rather enjoyed being alone. I didn't mind driving alone, spending the night in a hotel alone, or eating alone. I wasn't on vacation; I was a mom, determined to get to my son.

I'm convinced this woman in Mark Chapter 7 gave no thought to being alone; she had one goal on her mind – get to Jesus, now. As she and I learned, *later never happens.*

KEY POINT: EVIL IS NO RESPECTER OF PERSONS

The Prince of Darkness reigns on earth. And he owns and operates evil. He respects no one: male or female, young or old, rich or poor, introverted or extroverted, artistic or athletic, glad or gloomy, well-known or reclusive – he doesn't care. His role and goal are the same. He sets out to steal our strength, leaving us weary. He plots to kill our strength, leaving us weak. And he schemes to destroy our strength, leaving us worn out. We live in his territory; therefore, we aren't immune to his wiles.

The Light of the World reigns within His followers; therefore, we're owned and operated by the Father, His

Son, and the Holy Spirit. Jesus came to Satan's territory; He willingly left heaven and came to earth to save us from the *penalty of sin*. All who believe in Jesus and call on His Name and accept God's free gift of salvation are freed from the *power of sin*. However, because we dwell in the Devil's domain, we are not freed from the *presence of sin* until we reach heaven.

Satan's role is clear. And his goal continues to rampage the world. Evil is prevalent. Sin is rampant. And no one is exempt, including children.

Mark 7:25 says "…a woman whose little daughter was possessed by an evil spirit came and fell at his feet." Mark could have left the *little* adjective out. In the original language, the word for daughter denotes she's young. But Mark desired the reader get this detail.

Matthew also tells this woman's story. In Chapter fifteen of his gospel, Matthew's account differs slightly from Mark's interpretation. Mark tells us in his words what the woman said, while Matthew directly quotes her. In Matthew 15:22, I notice this momma and I have things in common. Yes, we're both mothers, but I surmise she's also passionate as she loudly portrays her emotion.

"A Canaanite woman…came to him, crying out, 'Lord, my daughter is suffering terribly from demon-possession." We read *crying* and we assume tears are present, evidencing the emotion. Understanding the original language tells us she loudly cried, shouting her concern for her little girl. Mark says her daughter is possessed by an evil spirit. Matthew adds the cry of this mother's heart: her little girl suffers terribly. The King James Version says, "…my daughter is grievously vexed with a devil."

The Greek meaning for *grievously vexed* conveys the girl is miserably, wrongly, and improperly possessed. This young daughter is under the power of a demon.

Messengers of Satan badger this little girl. She's possessed by spirits who are superior to humanity. Evil owns this girl. Mentally, it had a tight hold. Emotionally, it wouldn't let go. A straight jacket of evil clung and adhered to her, wrapping around her like a cloak.

Mark says, "...whose little daughter was possessed by an evil spirit..." The King James Version says she had an unclean spirit. The Greek word referring to the demon possession is echo. Yes, that's right. Echo. Our English word means a repetitive sound. The Greek word means to have, to hold, to possess the mind with agitating emotions.

And this momma has had enough. *Oh, no you don't. Not my daughter.* And she went into action. She bravely went to battle – dueling forces fighting for her daughter. Evil was holding on tight. Love and passion of a mother was evil's opponent. But love and passion from a parent aren't enough to reclaim this child from the grip of evil or a mother from the brink of despair.

KEY POINT: LOVE AND PASSION SHOULD USHER US TO THE FEET OF JESUS

The demons possessing this daughter are superior to humanity, but they're inferior to Deity. The feet of Jesus are a safety net for this mother. Followers of Jesus who fall at His feet are caught in His grip of love and grace. Fighting bravely for our people – our family and friends – infers we place them at the feet of Jesus. Facing evil alone is a futile effort. We can't battle Satan without Jesus.

In Mark 7:25 we see a woman fighting bravely for her child. Evil drove her to despair. Love and passion escorted her to the feet of Jesus. Resolute describes her will. A strong will is tenacious. A strong will perseveres. A strong will is steadfast. Her not-with-my-daughter-on-my-watch attitude is resolute. This mother is determined to get a face-to-face encounter with Jesus on behalf of her daughter. Ignorance and perhaps, stupidity, would have anyone stand in her way.

Nothing gets in the way of resolute. A woman determined to fall at the feet of Jesus can't be swayed. Oh, she may be delayed, but motivation keeps her steadfast on the path to Jesus.

"God demonstrates His own love for us in this: while we were still sinning, Christ died for us." Romans 5:8 points us to God's love for humanity. *Christ died for us.* It was the Father's plan, but Jesus demonstrates a passionate pursuit to obey His Father's will.

Followers of Jesus are motivated by love and passion because it was first demonstrated for us. This woman in Mark Chapter seven fell at the unscarred feet of Jesus. When we fall at His feet, His scars are a reminder of God's passionate love for us.

KEY POINT: BURDENS ARE LIFTED AT THE FOOT OF HIS CROSS

The Gospels record accounts of people falling at the feet of Jesus. And they tell of people gathering at the foot of His cross. I'm drawn to the cross every time I enter a sanctuary. I desire to see it lifted high and I long to see it empty, with no depiction of Christ hanging there. When He was pulled off the cross and placed in the tomb, He never went back to Calvary. Therefore, I love the empty cross because it points to resurrection, redemption, and renewal.

Though Jesus didn't return to Calvary, we can. And we must – because burdens are lifted at Calvary. As one hymn states, *Jesus is very near*. Mary, the mother of Jesus, was at the foot of the cross. She witnessed Calvary's love as she watched Jesus die. Portions of John 19:25-26 say, "Near the cross of Jesus stood his mother..." and "When Jesus saw his mother..."

Mary had eyes on her Savior, the Christ. Yes, she was His mother, but He didn't come to earth to be her son; He came to earth to save us all from the penalty of sin. On this hill called Mt. Calvary, Jesus hung wounded and bleeding on His cross. As He hung, those gathered at His feet clung to a hope they didn't understand. Just as Jesus lifted the burden of a Canaanite woman, He lifted Mary's burden, as well.

Mary was His mother, but she still needed to lay her burdens down at the feet of Jesus. The foot of the cross and the feet of Jesus bear all our burdens – if we lay them down. Mary, His mother and a determined Canaanite momma, trusted Jesus. Shouldn't we?

KEY POINT: JESUS CAN'T LIFT WHAT WE DON'T PLACE AT HIS FEET

The faith of this Canaanite woman landed her at the feet of Jesus. Desperation ignited her determination and drove this momma to the one she trusts can fight the waging battle on behalf of her daughter. Evil had a hold on the girl. And this momma holds on to hope. Her hope is named Jesus. She fell at His feet, placed her need there, and Jesus lifted her burden.

Does she wholly trust or does her trust bear holes?

A whole trust wholly trusts. Having faith in Jesus and placing our hope on Him implies we don't reclaim the burden. When we keep one hand and one eye on the burden, Jesus doesn't have complete control. To the follower of Jesus, partial surrender should be an oxymoron – the contradiction clouds the relinquishment. If Jesus isn't in complete control, then our faith has holes. And we live weary, weak, and worn out.

Be assured, Jesus is stronger than Satan's strong hold. When Satan has a grip, Jesus should have our attention. When the echoes of evil vie for our concentration, we must get our eyes fully on Jesus.

Satan has a tight hold on this girl and his voice reverberates inside her mind, causing agitation. But the fierce love of Jesus can infiltrate the strongholds and invade the echoes of the Devil.

Perhaps you have certain voices looping inside your mind, affecting your stance. How can we stand strong when the voices have weakened us? How can we remain firmly rooted in our faith when the voices make us weary? How can we fall at His feet if we're too worn out to get there? When the internal chaos detonates, we're an emotional, mental, and spiritual wreck.

KEY POINT: FOLLOWERS OF JESUS KNOW HIS VOICE

Indisputably, the Voice of Truth is stronger and much more proficient than the Father of Lies. Jesus is The Truth; therefore, His voice is to be trusted. Satan is a liar; therefore, he can't be trusted. In John 10:11, Jesus says of himself, "I am the Good Shepherd." It's paramount a shepherd makes sure the sheep recognize his voice.

In John 10:27, the Good Shepherd says, "My sheep listen to my voice; I know them, and they follow me." A shepherd is responsible for the welfare and safety of his flock. Leading the sheep to prime pastures, protecting the sheep from predators and poisonous plants, and providing for the sheep's needs allow the flock to survive and thrive.

In John 10:1, the Voice of Truth says, "I tell you the truth…" Do you trust His voice?

In John 10:3, Jesus says the sheep listen for His voice. Do you know His voice?

In John 10:4, the Good Shepherd says the sheep follow Him; they know His voice. Are you listening for His voice?

In John 10:14, Jesus continues, "…I know my sheep and my sheep know me."

Perhaps you have destructive, hurt-filled, discouraging voices echoing in the recesses of your mind. A boss declared you were fired. A friend hurled false accusations. A parent said you'd never amount to much. These unruly voices, deposited by negative influences, clamor for space in your memory bank. Some voices aren't loud; some come in whispered tones. But their path of destruction is imminent.

If you struggle to hear the voice of Jesus over the chaos, perhaps you need to fall at His feet and become reacquainted with His voice.

Though the Canaanite woman heard about Jesus, she's never heard His voice. But she's resolute in her desire to stop the devastating voices agitating her daughter. She's brave and determined to free her daughter from the grip of evil. Her determination to get to Jesus and her bravery to beg Jesus encourages us today.

Both my daughters have experienced negative voices causing a commotion of emotion in their hearts and minds. How can I be so sure? Because they breathe. No one is immune. My two girls bookend four sons. I have had reason to fall at the feet of Jesus on their behalf, begging and pleading for His counsel and intervention. As a mom, I know my kids are safest under His watchful care. I desire they be held by Him and led by Him.

Psalm 63:8 says, "My soul clings to you; your right hand upholds me." If my soul is clinging to the Lord, then I'm able to release my kids to Him.

Psalm 139:10 says, "Even there your hand will guide me, your right hand will hold me fast." God promises to guide and hold our kids.

Isaiah 41:13 says, "For I am the Lord, your God, who takes hold of your right hand…" God holds this mother, and He holds her daughter.

KEY POINT: WHEN JESUS TOUCHES YOUR NEED, YOUR HANDS ARE OFF

Once we lay our burdens down, they're no longer ours to hold. I know there have been many times I've pleaded and begged Jesus to intervene on issues. I've surrendered them to Him; I've relinquished control to Him. When it comes to laying my children at the feet of Jesus, I have a picture of God keeping His promise and taking hold of their right hand.

The same determination that brought the resolute woman in Mark Chapter seven to Jesus is the same resolve that keeps her hand off her daughter and her eyes on Jesus. The same determination that brought us to Jesus keeps our hands off the burden we laid down. Resolute remains firm even if the Voice of Truth is silent. Look at Matthew's account of what happened after this Canaanite woman cried out to Jesus and fell at His feet. Matthew 15:23 says, "Jesus did not answer a word…"

She's crossed over cultural standards, she's stepped out in faith, and she's laid her burden at the feet of the one she's only heard about. She's weary. She's weak. She's worn out. And Jesus has nothing to say?

Whoa. Hang on. That's not what Matthew's account

says. Jesus not answering her does not mean He has nothing to say. Every action, every word, every thought, and every motive of Jesus is first held by His Father and guided by the Holy Spirit. His silence isn't avoidance. His silence isn't Him ignoring her. His silence isn't unmerciful. And His followers shouldn't become undone in His silence. Jesus isn't done dealing with this mother – He's aware of all the needs surrounding her one plea.

Keeping our hands off our need keeps our focus on Jesus – even if we feel He isn't paying attention. Matthew 15:23 continues, "...So his disciples came to him and urged him, 'Send her away, for she keeps crying out after us."

Oh, how I love this titbit that proves her resoluteness: *She keeps crying out.* In her weakness, *she keeps crying out.* In her weariness, *she keeps crying out.* As she's worn out, *she keeps crying out.* And those closest to Jesus are annoyed, they've had enough, and they want Jesus to make her go away.

KEY POINT: WHEN GOD SEEMS SILENT, KEEP HANGING ON

His silence isn't for her. She fell at His feet, she placed her need there, and He lifted her burden. It's safely in His right hand, under His control. Obviously, His disciples are not. Jesus heard the cry of her heart; the disciples heard her cry. And they need their perspective altered.

The disciples took the silent interlude as an opportunity to boisterously speak their mind. And what was there came roaring out. *Make her stop, send her away* was their complaining cry regarding her pleading cries.

Matthew 15:24 records Jesus responding, "I was sent only to the lost sheep of Israel." [Don't miss the shepherd/sheep inference.] Let's go back to Mark 7:27.

Jesus breaks His silence by saying, "First, let the children eat all they want...for it is not right to take the children's bread and toss it to their dogs."

If ever there was a verse that needed clarifying, this is a contender. The reference of *children* and *their dogs* is for the Jewish people present in this exchange. Romans 1:16 helps us understand the words of Jesus. "I am not ashamed of the gospel, because it is the power of God for the salvation of everyone who believes: first for the Jew, then for the Gentile." God established a covenant relationship through the people called Israelites. Jesus Christ came through this Jewish bloodline.

God has always been the Deliverer of His people. He promised to never leave them, He said He'd never abandon them, and He said He'd always be with them. When Jesus was born, He was declared Emmanuel, which means God with us. The Gospel, or Good News, of Jesus is this:

- Sin caused a chasm between humanity and God.
- God provided the bridge to cross the great divide.
- Jesus was born a baby, to one day die on a cross.
- Only the blood of Jesus crosses out sin.
- Anyone who believes and accepts this gospel, crosses the bridge back to God.

Here in Mark 7:27, the cross hasn't happened. But the disciples should understand the children/dog analogy. When eating a meal, crumbs are dropped to the floor. The intended consumer missed the opportunity to feast on what was dropped, but their pet dog would now be satisfied with the neglected morsels. Jesus was silent because His disciples needed correcting. Yes, they are following Him. Yes, they are on a mission with Him. Yes, they had places to go, but Jesus wants His followers to know, at times, their plan may change to meet other needs.

This hurting mother responds, "Yes, Lord, but even the dogs eat the crumbs that fall from their master's table." In other words, *I'm waiting under the table, even though your words are for others, I will wait. I will trust your silence toward my request. I trust you know best. I trust a speck of your power to be enough. I've heard what it's done for others...oh, I don't want the whole meal, just a crumb of what you offer, which will satisfy and be sufficient to meet my desperate need.*

Then Jesus answered. He responds to her faith. "Woman, you have great faith! Your request is granted." [Matthew 15:28]

KEY POINT: GREAT FAITH, GREAT GOD, GREAT WITNESS

Followers of Jesus are on the scene, and they've witnessed her great faith. Jesus brings attention to it – not because of her, rather, due to our great God. And He deemed her request granted. The English Standard Version says, "Be it done for you as you desire."

She must remain rooted in this newfound faith because she needs to return home to her daughter. This mother had no proof her daughter was well, but followers of Jesus shouldn't depend on what we know; we must walk by faith. Great faith in a great God will carry her home.

The Voice of Truth said her request was granted. He declared the daughter instantly cured. Matthew 15:28 concludes, "And her daughter was healed from that very hour." Mark's rendition says, "She went home and found her child lying on the bed, and the demon gone." (Mark

7:30)

Jesus never laid a hand on the little girl, yet His power still entered her young life. A resolute woman had great faith that Jesus could make demons flee so her child could become demon free. And a resolute woman, filled with great faith, returned home and witnessed something she hadn't experienced in a while. Peace.

Consider her life before she left home. Contemplate the commotion of emotion exploding from her daughter before she pursued a face-to-face encounter with Jesus. The demonic echoes clamoring inside this girl's mind would need an escape route. Those around knew the eruption was imminent; however, with no forewarning, the reverberating voices would explode out of the little girl. And the runoff would cause witnesses to flee.

KEY POINT: VERBAL RUN-OFF CAUSES OTHERS TO RUN OFF

Recently, Hawaii experienced mass destruction from the eruption of the Kilauea volcano. As I write this, the latest eruption cycle continues to spew what's been rumbling inside the cone. Since 1983, there's been volcanic activity. Even so, life went on for the people living nearby. People purchased homes, maintained properties, and settled in – aware of the eruption, but never knowing when or if it would explode.

Today, as I write, hundreds are homeless, wildlife is obliterated, rivers of lava continue to flow in destructive paths, ash pollutes the air, and chemicals affect the ocean. A quick glimpse at a headline pronounces, "...five weeks of unprecedented turmoil and destruction, with no end in sight..."

A volcano is a vent in the earth where dangerous

matter escapes – a runoff of disastrous and perilous proportions. After all, what's inside must get released. Like the little girl in Mark Chapter seven, there may be an eruption inside you. At times, it finds an escape route. Other times, it's simmering or smoldering – a suppressed combustion, powerless to hold down. Bitter attitudes and unforgiving spirits threaten to explode. There's angry, cutting, ugly, nasty, hurt-filled, divisive words echoing in your head. Perhaps you've been cruelly and verbally abused. The vile echoes reverberate deep inside, and eventually they need a way out.

Volatile emotions and verbal eruptions keep us weary, weak, and worn out. The runoff wounds our character and harms relationship. Followers of Jesus – the evil echoes need to run off, not our family and friends.

We need a face-to-face encounter with Jesus. We must become resolute and trust the Prince of Peace with our internal chaos. It's imperative we bring our desperate selves to Jesus, fall at His feet, and courageously ask Jesus to calm all internal distress.

KEY POINT: RESOLUTE FIGHTS BRAVELY FOR THEIR PEOPLE

My people are not your people. It is possible persons may overlap; however, each group is unique. In 2 Samuel 10, Joab, one of King David's military leaders, along with his troops, face a certain battle. Joab is determined to stand his ground and defend his land. Joab is strong, courageous, and firm. He looks the part, and he lives it out. He grew into this position – he prevailed through difficulty and hardship and earned the role of leader.

Though the enemy has Joab's army hemmed in, Joab is resolute. He's all in for battle. 2 Samuel 10:12 records

Joab taking a courageous stance alongside his men and encourages them to "Be strong and let us fight bravely for our people and the cities of our God. The Lord will do what is good in his sight." In the original language, *be strong* and *fight bravely* are the same Hebrew word. Joab tells his people to prevail, be strong, be firm, be courageous, press in, be secure, take a bold stance, and fight – bravely fight because what they're fighting for matters; facing the battle is worth the fight.

This mother is Mark Chapter seven bravely fights for her daughter. She prevailed, she stood firm, she pressed in and boldly approached Jesus on behalf of her daughter. One of her people was in a battle, the enemy had her daughter hemmed in, and she stood her ground and bravely remained in the fight.

When fighting for our people, Lamentations 2:19 contains a battle plan. "*Arise, cry* out in the night...*pour out* your heart...in the presence of the Lord. *Lift up your hands* to him..."

Arise	a woman came to Jesus
Cry out	crying out to Him
Pour out your heart	her daughter suffered terribly of demon possession
Lift up your hands	she relinquished her burden to Jesus

The battle plan ends with "...for the lives of your children, who faint from hunger..." At times, our people will be weary, weak, and worn out. Their hungry hearts need to be satisfied. As followers of Jesus, we know the one who satisfies.

My people need me, and your people need you, to fight bravely and be strong. Standing strong requires we stand resolute, determined to courageously endure all battles until all our people are face to face with Jesus.

PONDER

deeply, carefully, and thoughtfully consider

1. What is your definition of brave?

2. How can you fight bravely for your people? (2 Samuel 10:12)

3. Who do you consider to be a brave hero? Why?

PERSUADE

God's Word influences, encourages, and guides

1. Mark 7:25 shares two important facts that influenced this woman to a face-to-face encounter with Jesus. What are they?

    a. she _____ about Him

    b. she _____ at His _____

2. How does God demonstrate His love for us? (Romans 5:8)

3. How are you encouraged by the following verses?

    a. John 10:27

    b. Psalm 63:8

    c. Psalm 139:10

    d. Isaiah 41:13

4. Based on Lamentations 2:19 write out a battle plan to fight bravely for your people.

PRACTICAL

applying Biblical Truth to present day

1. Everyone has opportunity to affect a child's spiritual foundation. According to Proverbs 22:6, what can you do to apply this truth in your life?

2. Read John 19:25-26.

   a. Where is Jesus?

   b. Where is Mary?

   Consider a difficulty you're currently experiencing.

   c. Where is Jesus?

   d. Where are you?

3. In Matthew 15:28 Jesus affirms a resolute woman and He tells her what He will do for her. Focus on the affirmation. What does He say?

   Woman,

   _____

   _____

4. Read the following verses. How can your faith in God increase as you face uncertainty?

    a. Romans 4:19-20

    b. Isaiah 7:9

    c. Habakkuk 2:4

    d. Romans 1:12

    e. 1 Corinthians 16:13

PERSONAL
inviting Jesus into your current reality

1. Fighting bravely is hard work.

    a. Are you standing strong?

    b. If not, what can you do? If yes, what will you continue to do?

2. Do you have a strong individual fighting for you? (If no, pray and ask God to provide this person. Write out the prayer below.)

    a. Who is it?

    b. What makes them the right person to fight bravely for you?

6
strength for the TENUOUS

"And the God of all grace, who called you to his eternal glory in Christ, after you have suffered a little while, will himself restore you and make you strong, firm, and steadfast."
1 Peter 5:10

I can remember a certain game we played in elementary school. The teacher would gather us in a circle and create a situational scenario. Taking turns, we'd go around the circle and share our answer to one question. Though the scenarios changed, the question remained the same: What two items would you choose to take with you?

Scenario: You're going to a deserted island to write.
Question: What two items do you take?
Answer: My Bible and a thesaurus.

At times, as I write, my thoughts can lack substance, become weak, and remain vague. I need my Bible – it's my choice when seeking foundational truth, guidance, and wisdom. God's Word strengthens my faith and brings clarity to beliefs, opinions, and thoughts.

Along with my Bible, I'm taking a thesaurus to the island. Sometimes while writing, my word choices become limited and need variety. Other times they lack affect and need expression.

As I write this, I'm not on a deserted island but at our summer place. Sitting near me are two resources, my Bible and my tablet. The electronic device would be of no use on a deserted island and since our home away from home doesn't have internet connection, it's invaluable to the task at hand. With cellular data, in a few easy steps I can quickly access multiple translations of the Bible, the Hebrew and Greek definitions, Bible commentaries, Bible encyclopedias, a dictionary, and of course, the thesaurus.

Today, before I started writing, I researched, studied, and pondered looking for a suitable focus word to use as the theme for chapter six. I read and re-read Mark 8:22-25, the Scriptural base. I also studied and reflected on 1 Peter 5:10, the correlating verse for this chapter. After a lengthy exploration and many word inspections in the thesaurus, the chapter theme was revealed through an uncommon word. *Tenuous.*

According to dictionaries, the definition for tenuous is unstable, weak, and lacking clarity. The tenuous one needs strength. For the unstable, weak, and unsettled follower, only a face-to-face encounter with Jesus provides stability, strength, and a settled soul.

Mark is the only gospel writer to tell this story of the blind man at Bethsaida. As I read and re-read about his face-to-face encounter with Jesus (Mark 8:22-25), I was unsettled and felt the story was weak and lacked what I was seeking to accomplish in this chapter.

Thankfully, Paul's wisdom in 2 Timothy 3:16 proved true. It says God's Word is useful for teaching, correcting, rebuking, and training in righteousness. I needed correcting. The Holy Spirit trained me up in righteousness and taught me significant life lessons from this little story about a blind man's encounter with Jesus.

A strong-willed woman has difficulty describing herself as tenuous. *I am not unstable. I am not weak. And I'm certainly not lacking clarity.* And don't even think about accusing me of such things. Yes, a strong-will easily turns stubborn. But God's spirit is stalwart. His still, small voice invaded my obstinacy.

"Ellen, what about _____?" God asked. Immediately, I knew to what He was referring. This current situation has me blinded, and His revelation shows me I'm weary, I'm weak, and I'm worn-out.

I can't avoid it any longer – I'm tenuous and in need of His strength.

KEY POINT: WE'RE BLINDED BY WHAT HAS OUR ATTENTION

Have you ever had an issue so consume you that it was all you could focus on? Has something grabbed your attention, determining your emotional state? Has the situation wound its way into many conversations? Are you so blinded by a certain issue, you make sure the trusted confidants and prayer warriors in your life have marked it in ink on their prayer list?

Oh, there's nothing wrong with praying for the consuming issues. In fact, there's everything right about it. But, right can go wrong when we're exhausted and frenzied from our concerns – swayed by their power and persuaded by the control they have over our life.

Years ago, as my husband was driving home from a funeral of a colleague, he called with a concern. "Ellen, I'm experiencing something weird. As I was sitting in the funeral service, I looked at the cross and the vertical beam appeared to slightly curve." He went on to say how days earlier road signs seemed to be distorted, but thinking it was a one-time instance, he never mentioned it.

My immediate thoughts weren't positive. But I quickly went into action. I hung up with Kevin and called our family physician. He confirmed my thoughts. "Ellen, you need to get Kevin to the Emergency Room right away. I'll call ahead and initiate things."

Moments later, Kevin pulled in the driveaway, I hopped in the driver's seat and drove to the hospital. Less than 90 minutes later, Kevin was triaged, assessed by the ER doctor, and sent for a CT scan of his head. The result was a good news/bad news report. Good news: No brain tumor. Bad news: His eyesight was worsening. What he was used to seeing in color was quickly graying and blurring. The ER physician called a local ophthalmologist, a doctor treating anatomy, function, and disease of the eye, who was waiting at his office for us to arrive.

After that exam, we had answers. Blood vessels had found pathways through holes in Kevin's retina field, depositing blood and fluid into his field of vision, distorting his eyesight. Though the holes didn't surprise us, the distortion had.

A couple of years earlier, Kevin went to an informative meeting to begin the process of having a procedure that would potentially improve his severe near-sightedness. Through the initial screening, he was told about the holes and we were advised any corrective procedure was no longer an option for Kevin.

I remember being dumbfounded in that initial screening room. After the optometrist matter-of-factly told Kevin his poor vision could not be helped, he opened a drawer, retrieved a sheet of paper off a tall stack, and said, "You have ocular histoplasmosis syndrome." According to this doctor and the stack of papers in that exam room drawer, Kevin was one of many who at one time in his life was infected by a common fungus. We learned air born spores found near certain river valleys get transferred when certain creatures of the feathered community poop in the soil. Plowing or digging the soil releases the spores into the air, causing a virus.

The doctor went on to say most people would test positive for this syndrome, but their immune systems successfully fought off what masked as a common cold. Kevin is in the minority. His immune system didn't fight off the virus, and eventually it affected his eyesight. We were not properly prepared for the day Kevin's eyesight went haywire. Looking back, we wished the optometrist wouldn't have nonchalantly communicated the news that later had us tenuous. However, remaining stuck in past wouldn't correct Kevin's vision.

When Kevin experienced those radical changes, it was because the abnormal blood vessels were depositing fluid into his central vision path and answered the question why straight lines became curvy and crooked and color began to distort.

A retina specialist became his new doctor, many laser procedures occurred, and months later, a last-ditch-effort surgery was scheduled to potentially restore the lost vision. Today, even though the peripheral is intact, Kevin has no center-vision in his left eye. The thickness in the lenses of his glasses prove Kevin's severe near-sightedness. He is completely dependent on corrective eyewear. Because he wears contact lenses, people are ignorant of my husband's vision challenges.

The one eye surgery had a 25% chance of restoring some vision, but it wasn't successful.

As I write this, fifteen years have passed since the cross appeared crooked, the color was distorted, and his vision diminished. Kevin's partial blindness still affects him and at times can have his attention. Though he has never complained, he certainly has concern. Regular check-ups with eye doctors, daily eyedrops to help keep the pressure down, and avoiding potentially dangerous activity protect the vision that remains.

Hard circumstances in our life have us tenuous. They quickly get our attention and can make us take our eyes off Jesus while distorting and diminishing our faith.

KEY POINT: UNABLE CAN LEAD TO UNSTABLE

God opened my eyes to the fact I'm tenuous. I realize my spiritual vision has been distorted. This current difficulty has messed with my faith. And, I'm hesitant to admit, has me unstable, weak, and unsettled. I'm unable to step aside from the instability. I'm crushed by the weight of the burden as it takes up more and more emotional and mental space. All options toward solution have been exhausted – I'm blank; unable to think of further recourse. I'm short-tempered, impatient, and unfocused.

I'm weary, weak, and worn out. I'm blinded by what has my attention. Other areas of my life are unstable where stability used to be the norm. Doubt has become common, weariness looms, weakness appears, and exhaustion settles. I'm unable to see beyond this current reality. Lord, please help!

+ +

Six weeks have passed since I cried out to the Lord. I'm not sure if this is true for all writers and speakers, but every lesson I write on, preach about, or teach to others, God makes sure I experience. As I said, I struggled to connect this story in Mark 8:22-25 to the theme of this chapter because I failed to listen when God attempted to get my attention to alter the title. Months before writing began, I outlined this book and had a different title for chapter six.

I didn't like admitting I was tenuous. Unstable, weak, and unsettled are not words that describe my character or personality. But they accurately described my spiritual condition these past few weeks. If we're not careful, instability has us believe we're not spiritually healthy until the big dilemmas go away. And that's a lie!

The story of this blind man in Mark Chapter eight, combined with 1Peter 5:10, have taught me how to stand strong, rather than being crushed by any struggle, including my current reality. 1Peter 5:10 begins, "And the God of all grace, who called you to his eternal glory in Christ, after you have suffered a little while…"

Pause.
After you have suffered a little while

Deep breath.
Exhale.

It's a fact – followers of Jesus will suffer. Fifteen times in the first of two letters, Peter mentions suffering in one form or another. Living godly doesn't dwell on easy street. But Christians can easily get blindsided when trouble comes to the door.

There's a difference between:

thinking something has us tenuous

and

the Lord *assigning/allowing* tenuous situations.

We can get so focused on what's causing us to suffer that we neglect seeing God in the suffering. Followers must be careful when circumstances have us unstable, weak, and unsettled. Consumed by weariness and weakness doesn't stand strong. When we live under difficult circumstances, we misstep on our faith journey. When we're deceived to believe what we think is true, tenuousness can overshadow truth.

But what happens if our perspective changes? What if tenuous situations are allowed by God? What if He assigns suffering which causes tenuousness? We're able to stand strong through the tenuous moments when we're walking by faith and fully trusting the Lord.

For six weeks as I sat down to work on this chapter, I had nothing – no words, no inspiration. During these weeks, I sought guidance through the counsel and wisdom of two friends. They encouraged me, listened to me, prayed for me, and supported me. But they also helped correct my vision to get me back on the right path.

God used these women to show me I was focused on the circumstance instead of fixed on Jesus. They guided me through this challenging time that had me tenuous and spiritually unstable, weak, and unsettled.

KEY POINT: TENUOUS ISN'T ALWAYS WAYWARD

Proverbs 3:6 says, "In all your ways, acknowledge Him, and He will make your paths straight." Because my friends love me, they cared enough to correct me. They didn't want this situation to blind me from seeing Jesus. They could tell I was weary, weak, and worn out. They didn't focus on praying my situation away; rather, they prayed I would acknowledge God, seek His presence, and stand firm. Before they wanted my situation improved, they desired I walk by faith and get back on the straight path God promises. They reminded me that when suffering, God never abandons His children. Trusting God in tenuous situations, assures us His presence will be present whether the circumstance changes or not.

Getting my weak eyes off my weary situation opened my mind and heart for the Holy Spirit to inspire my writing. I studied, wrote some notes, poured over this story about the blind man at Bethsaida, and connected the lessons learned to my current reality. Though the tenuous situation hasn't changed, I have. And I'm ready to write about strength for the tenuous.

+ +

Five weeks have passed since I wrote that last sentence. It was a Friday night, and I was thanking God for His restoring power. He made me strong, firm, and steadfast. I remember wanting to continue writing but decided to go to bed and opt for an early start the next day. I set my alarm and slept peacefully. Though that difficult situation remained, the internal suffering was eased and controlled. God's strength had restored my weary, weak, or worn-out heart.

God's promise rang true: *After you have suffered a little while, [God] will Himself restore you and make you strong, firm, and steadfast.*

A phone call from my mom's doctor woke me before the alarm. "Ellen, your mom is unresponsive. We're not sure why, but she's been moved to ICU. Your family should get here as soon as possible."

Mom had been in the hospital for days to help manage lower back pain from a bulged disc. An unrelated issue arose necessitating a quick procedure which had been scheduled for later that Saturday before they could move her to an in-patient physical therapy location.

The uninvited and shocking news brought a new suffering into my life. Writing was set aside as plans were put in motion to meet my dad and sisters at the hospital.

As I left our summer place and started the two-hour journey, I drove in silence. I wasn't panicked; I wasn't worried. I was concerned and confused. I tried to pray, but words wouldn't form, and I wasn't bothered by their absence. God sees hearts; therefore, wordless prayers are not empty thoughts to God. He hears the silent prayers of a sincere heart.

A short and simple assertion from God entered the quiet and steadied any uncertainty. "Be still and know that I am God…" This declaration from Psalm 46:10 is an imperative promise for the tenuous follower to hold on to. The stillness surrounding my vehicle made me more aware of God's presence. In the silence, His promise soothed my soul.

In the stillness, I sensed weariness, but I was anchored by His presence. In the silence, awareness dawned. The voice of God wasn't audible, but the message and meaning were understood.

KEY POINT: TENUOUS NEEDS AN ANCHOR

My child, you are about to understand what strength for the tenuous truly means. You're about to face a suffering that will bring the lessons to fruition that I have been writing on your heart. Pay careful attention. Keep your eyes on Me. I am your strength.

God's still, small voice spoke. Had I been running my mouth with words of doubt, questions demanding answers, or unchecked bursts of emotion, I would have missed how steady one can be when anchored by God's strength through deep suffering. It would not have been well with my soul.

At 8:00 Saturday morning, a team of doctors took mom from the ICU and into the operating room to stop an infection revealed through a CT scan. Three hours later, we were baffled by the surgeon's explanation. A flesh-eating infection had quickly invaded mom's bloodstream, and her situation was very grim. Though the surgeon was able to get ahead of the infection, her physiology was precariously poor.

Thirty-seven hours later, two incidents simultaneously occurred. Mom took her last breath and came face-to-face with Jesus. Mom will never know pain and suffering again. Her flesh died, but her soul lives on. Mom is face to face with her Savior for eternity.

Losing my mom has me tenuous. When weary, weak, and worn out are my reality, Jesus is my anchor. Over the past five weeks, I've been physically weak and emotionally unsettled and unstable. But spiritually, I have remained strong, firm, and steadfast. God promises He'll be an ever-present help in times of trouble. (Psalm 46:1) God's Word says He'll keep us safe through trouble. (Psalm 27:5) We're guaranteed He'll be our refuge in distress, a shelter in the storm, and shade from the heat. (Isaiah 25:4) I know these promises are true.

When tenuous, we're prone to wander, inclined to leave the safety of God's protection. Through suffering, He desires to anchor us on the straight path He establishes as we acknowledge His presence and wholeheartedly trust His ways.

KEY POINT: TENUOUS SITUATIONS TEACH VALUABLE LESSONS

In His great mercy, God had allowed the other challenging issue in my life to teach me how to react and respond to this new storm that blew uninvited and unexpected into my life. He provided my friends who helped rescue me from my wayward mindset due to the mishandling of the previous tenuous circumstance. In His faithfulness, God prepared me to face losing my mom.

Followers of Jesus are not immune to unstable, weak, and unsettled circumstances or situations. Had I remained spiritually unstable, spiritually weak, and spiritually unsettled, I would have missed all God had for me in the tenuous moments. Avoiding or questioning tenuousness keeps us ignorant to the valuable lessons God has in store for His children.

The blind man at Bethsaida from Mark 8:22-25 is an example to the tenuous follower how to stand strong when struggles, crises, and trouble have us spiritually blind. Four specific words from the 1 Peter passage encourage and prepare us to stand strong.

"But the God of all grace, who hath called us unto His eternal glory by Christ Jesus,
after that ye have suffered a while,
RESTORE, STABLISH, STRENGTHEN, and SETTLE you."
1 Peter 5:10, King James Version

VALUABLE LESSON #1
RESTORE THE BROKEN

In Mark 8:22 we're introduced to the blind man. "They came to Bethsaida, and some people brought a blind man and begged Jesus to touch him." The blind man was ignorant to his brokenness, so the people helped him get face to face with Jesus. Some people bring others to

Jesus because they're blinded to their own brokenness, pretend they're broken, or avoid and ignore the brokenness. Others refuse to be restored – they'd rather figure out how to manage the holes, rather than Jesus make them whole.

Allow me to introduce you to Bill and Ruth, who I met when they were in their 80s. Bill and Ruth met Jesus on the same day when they were in their 40s. A neighbor had invited Ruth to a revival service – a series of meetings separate from regular Sunday morning worship gatherings. Revival services are a valuable opportunity for active church members to bring their unsaved friends to hear about the Gospel of Jesus Christ. Bill heard Ruth was going, so he decided to tag along. Ruth was aware of her brokenness; Bill was ignorant to his.

During the message, Bill fell asleep. As the preacher concluded, an invitation was given. The people were persuaded to bring their brokenness to the altar and turn their lives over to Jesus. Ruth bolted out of her pew and began her trek to the altar. Bill woke up as Ruth stood up. He followed his wife, oblivious to the invitation and ignorant to the destination. It wasn't until they stood at the altar that Bill realized they weren't leaving the sanctuary.

As Bill tells it, he says, "I figured if it was good enough for my Ruth, it was good enough for me." Bill and Ruth both needed their lives restored. One was aware, the other unaware. One listened with rapt attention, the other unconscious through the sermon. Restoration doesn't look the same in everyone. Yet, Bill and Ruth had one thing in common – each needed a face-to-face encounter with Jesus.

From that day on, Bill and Ruth followed Jesus. He changed them completely. He restored their purpose and perspective. And it all began because someone brought Ruth to Jesus.

The people begged Jesus to touch the blind man. The word for touch means to adhere to or cling to. Some people love the broken people in their lives well enough to beg Jesus for an encounter on their behalf. Some people trust Jesus to handle broken pieces in their friends' lives.

This man is blind. Not only does it refer to physical blindness, but this word can also mean to be mentally blind. Bill, like the blind man, was mentally blind – he was unaware of his brokenness which blinded him spiritually.

The man at Bethsaida is physically and mentally and spiritually blind. He needs his sight restored.

VALUABLE LESSON #2
STABLISH THE UNSTABLE

Peter says after we've suffered a little while, God will stablish us, or make us strong. When we're weary, weak, and worn out, we're unstable. And unstable is unable to stand strong.

When I was 19, I started working at a car dealership as the administrative assistant to the body shop manager. I wasn't expected to know about vehicles. That was a good thing because I was ignorant. Answering the phones, greeting customers, filing repair orders, and overseeing the supply inventory were my main responsibilities. But it didn't take long for me to pay close attention as the manager wrote estimates on damaged cars.

As I learned the process of repairing and restoring vehicles back to their intended use, ignorance turned to awareness. It didn't take long, and I was promoted to the assistant manager position. I didn't know how to fix the broken vehicles, but I knew who could. It always amazed me to watch the professional repairmen take broken pieces, twisted and bent frames, smashed bumpers, crushed and mangled sheet metal and restore the unstable back to its intended use.

Within the suspension system of a vehicle is the stabilizer bar. It keeps the vehicle steady on curves, large bumps, and sharp corners. It's unwise to drive with a broken stabilizer. Though the car is drivable, loose steering and vehicle sway compromise the overall function.

Jesus is our stabilizer. When we're swayed by troubling circumstances, we need to be stablished. We need Jesus. After the people begged Jesus to touch the blind man, "He took the blind man by the hand and led him…" (Mark 8:23a)

- Jesus took charge
- Jesus took hold
- Jesus took the lead

This encounter wasn't happenstance. Being stablished requires knowing who's in charge. The people pleaded, almost demanded that Jesus touch him, but it's Jesus who initiated. A holy and eternal God is at work in this world. At times He uses people to connect to people. This blind man has an appointment ordained by God to connect with Jesus.

This man is unstable – unable to see, unable to work, unable to function well – his existence was arduous. Unstable was his normal until the people took him to Jesus and Jesus took charge.

At that time, it was common for the blind to beg at the entrance of a city. They would sit on their cloaks with a bowl attached by a long cord around their waist. As people approached, they'd toss the bowl to the edge of the cloak and yank it back as soon as something landed in the bowl. Hidden pockets kept the begging revenue safe. The cloak also served as a boundary marker to keep a blind man from wandering away or scooting off. The cloak was their comfort zone, a place of safety and security.

When do you think someone last touched the blind man? Yes, the people brought him to Jesus, but that doesn't mean they touched him. Some believed blindness was the result of a curse. That was reason enough to avoid a blind person. Not Jesus – He took hold of the blind man. Holding his hand, Jesus steadied the unstable man. Oh, there's power in the touch of Jesus.

Taking his hand, Jesus took charge and led the blind man. Where they were headed wasn't priority, it was enough to be led by a trusted source. From the blind man's perspective, someone else is in charge, and there's a freedom in this new reality. The text doesn't give detail, but it appears the blind man had no time or thought to gather his cloak, bowl, and begging revenue. When Jesus took hold, He also took the lead, and like the disciples this blind man left everything to be led by Jesus.

KEY POINT: GODLY NONSENSE MAKES SENSE

At times, through our human understanding, what we know to be God's plan appears to be nonsense. As He spoke in parables, people were confused. Even His disciples couldn't comprehend everything He taught them in the three years they followed Him. And there were perplexing times as Jesus performed miracles and communicated expectations.

Like the time Jesus told a lame man to get up and walk – that would bemuse and bewilder a crowd. Or when a crowd was pressed in, shoulder to shoulder, all around

Him and Jesus asked who touched Him – that seems absurd. And it appeared ridiculous when He told His disciples to prepare a boy's Happy Meal and feed the massive crowd of over 5000 hungry people.

In Mark 8:23 we read what seems silly and senseless. "...[he] led him outside the village. When Jesus had spit on the man's eyes..."

When I was a little girl, I recall my mom proceeding as if there was nothing wrong with licking her finger and removing a smudge on my face with her spit. There's *everything* wrong with that! I vowed I'd never do that to my children. Instead, I made them lick my finger and use their own spit to remove smudges from their faces.

He spit on the man's eyes? That's nonsense! The guy couldn't even see it coming. This unstable blind man is looking for stability. He's broken and needs to be restored. He's searching for purpose, for his life to make sense, and Jesus spits on the man's eyes? No wonder He led the blind man outside the village.

I'm not a grammar geek, but I do like an amusing onomatopoeia – when a word sounds like what it means. Sizzle, bam, and splat are all great examples. The Greek word for spit is *ptuo*. One on-line resource shows the definition, the phonetic spelling, and includes a microphone icon to hear the pronunciation. It's quite possible I may have pressed the mic symbol for *ptuo* more times than necessary. Phonetically, it's ptoó -o.

Reading on in Mark 8:23. "...[He] put His hands on him and asked, 'Do you see anything?" First, He spits on the man and now He asks a blind man if he can see. The nonsense keeps piling up. Why did Jesus put His hands on the blind man? Was it to keep him from running away? Or was the Healer stablishing the unstable?

To stand strong in this world, through difficulties and

brokenness, we cannot lean on our own understanding. (Proverbs 3:5) We remain unstable when we try to figure out why and how God operates. We're unable to see God's ways, His straight path, His healing and restoring power when we're stuck at *that just doesn't make sense.* Spiritual blindness will keep us in our comfort zones, never moving away from our man-made, self-proclaimed safety nets and security plans.

The trials and trouble of life blind us from seeing Jesus. Perhaps we need Him to spit on us and remove the smudges that keep us from seeing His purpose and plan.

We go to Him often asking for healing, searching for purpose, pleading to be made well, begging for His stability. Jesus is waiting for our answer to the same question He asked the blind man. "Do you see anything?"

KEY POINT: HAZY VISION NEEDS THE GREAT PHYSICIAN

Get your eyes off your circumstances and look around. There's no doubting My presence, you know I'm here, you can feel My touch. Open your eyes and see Me. It's the circumstances that have you unstable. I'm ready to steady you. Allow Me to exam your body, mind, and soul.

The Healer knew there was more to heal than just the blind man's eyes. The eyes of his heart required a touch from the Great Physician before the eyes on his face needed to work. It wasn't his broken eyes that had him unstable. Spiritual blindness and spiritual haziness have eternal consequences.

Distorted vision was the first sign my husband's eyesight was in jeopardy. Fifteen years later and this issue can easily grab his attention. My athletic husband is no longer the first-rate infielder on the church softball team.

Oh, his batting average and his base running are above average, but he is not able to accurately judge a line drive, an infield pop-up, or a fly ball to the outfield.

Kevin also exceled at table tennis. To the novice, it's ping-pong – to my husband it's a fast-paced, action-filled sport requiring precise perception. The loss of Kevin's center vision compromised his ability to compete at the same level before the effects of the virus tarnished his vision. Intact center vision allows for accurate depth perception.

Unbroken eye contact with Jesus stabilizes us with clear spiritual vision.

Jesus has asked the blind man a question. "Do you see anything?" With Jesus' spit on his face, the man looks up and says, "...I see people; they look like trees walking around." The man can see! A blind man has sight. Yes, it's fuzzy, but still. Wait. We cannot move on. We still need clarity on a couple of things.

First, when Mark 8:24 says *he looked up*, it literally means his lost sight was recovered. Yes, this blind man could sing the line from a famous hymn, "was blind, but now I see" and mean it two ways: physically and spiritually. But he can't sing a popular phrase from another tune and mean it: "I can see clearly now!" His sight might be restored, but he's looking through a haze.

Second, the man's response should have us asking two questions.

1. How does a blind man know what people look like?
2. How does a blind man know what trees look like?

This man had no vision, but his other senses were working fine. When I was a child, I attended church with a girl who was blind. I remember as new kids came, Michele would touch their faces. It was her way of becoming familiar with them. I imagine the blind man in Mark Chapter eight. He knew what people and trees looked like because he was familiar with their shapes and contours. Putting his arms around a tree trunk may have reminded him of when he hugged family members.

A blind man would be content to see through a fog, but those of us with 20/20 vision would not. A brand-new, born-again, saved follower of Jesus is excited, peaceful, joyful, and content with her eternal destination and newfound relationship with her Savior. But years later, spiritual enlightenment, spiritual growth, spiritual depth should be what they see, know, and rely on to live as followers of Jesus.

If brand-new believers never grew in their relationship with God, they'd live their days through a spiritual haze. And that's not living as Jesus intends.

VALUABLE LESSON #3
ONLY JESUS STRENGTHENS WEAK VISION

KEY POINT: HAZY DAYS MAKE US WEAK

We're easily led astray by what we *think* is true. Illusion. Deceived by production of a false reality. Hallucination. Misled through an impression of reality. Fantasy. Conjuring up unrealities to fulfill a need. Mirage. Deceived by phenomenon. Things aren't always as they appear. Living life in a haze will weaken us. Tenuous Christians are weak followers.

According to 1Peter 5:10, God stablishes and strengthens us. That's good news for the weak one living in hazy days. This kind of strength can't help you carry more groceries into the house. It won't build muscle tissue. Even better, the Great Physician does soul therapy. This promise from Peter says God strengthens suffering souls.

The blind man was a weak man. In his weakness, he would have lived the rest of his days through a haze, believing it was better than not seeing at all. In John 10:10, Jesus speaks a promise to His followers. "I have come that they may have life, AND have it to the full." [emphasis mine]

The blind man had new life – and he felt it, he loved it, he was ecstatic. But Jesus had more for him. He knows his new life is eternal life, but this blind man was still living on earth and the world is a crazy, hazy place. Jesus didn't just come to save people, He came to strengthen us, too.

The once blind man is now a weak man. And Jesus doesn't want this man to leave in a haze. So, the Healer touches the man's weakness. Mark 8:25 says, "Once more, Jesus put His hands on the man's eyes..."

KEY POINT: JESUS WANTS TO GET HIS HANDS ON YOU

Some people might think the spit thing didn't work. Well, just because you think it doesn't make it true. Things aren't always what they appear to be. Deity isn't dense or dumb. Everything God allows has eternal purpose. Jesus doesn't have ineffective spit. The blind man needed his soul strengthened. Having his initial vision distorted showed him he needed a touch from Jesus.

Jesus loves us so much, He wants to get His hands on us. Any touch from Jesus is a purposeful touch. For the blind man, the initial touch of spit gave him sight, stablishing and strengthening him. When Jesus put His hands on the man, He settled him.

VALUABLE LESSON #4
AN UNSETTLED SOUL NEEDS SETTLING

Tenuous followers lack clarity. Though his vision was restored, he was still in a haze. Standing strong can't live unsettled. Too many followers settle for a partially healed soul leaving them unsettled. Jesus desires to make us whole. The healed man needed what we all need – clear vision and clarity of soul. Mark 8:25 continues, "…Then his eyes were opened, his sight was restored, and he saw everything clearly."

There are slight differences in two versions of this passage.

NIV	KJV
+ Then his eyes were opened	+ Jesus made him look up
+ His sight was restored	+ He was restored
+ He saw everything clearly	+ He saw every man clearly

The phrases *looked up* (NIV) in Mark 8:24 and *made him look up* (KJV) in Mark 8:25 are the same original word. The implication is that the man didn't open his own eyes and he couldn't restore his own vision. Jesus recovered the man's sight and activated his spiritual vision.

Suffering comes through different avenues: broken friendships, financial burdens, health crises, hurting marriages, wayward children, emotional turmoil, and past demons, just to name a few. Every struggle can spiritually blind us, making us tenuous. Suffering unsettles us. When we lack clarity, we need Jesus to reclaim, restore, and resettle us.

When Jesus activated the man's vision, he saw everything, every man clearly. Literally, it means the man could see clearly now. Metaphorically, he was clear-minded, able to clearly consider everything. Jesus didn't make him smarter, He cleared the spiritual haze and settled his soul.

Unsettled has us anxious, upset, disconcerted, uneasy, troubled, tense, flustered, and tenuous. We're in need of Jesus activating our spiritual vision. When unsettled, our soul vision needs to be examined by the Great Physician. Don't delay! Make an appointment with the Healer who is able to restore, stablish, strengthen, and settle all who are tenuous.

PONDER

deeply, carefully, and thoughtfully consider

1. What causes you to be tenuous. Consider the following questions.

    a. In what ways are you unsteady?

    b. How has it made you weak?

    c. Where are you lacking clarity?

2. Tenuous situations may not change. How can you remain strong through tenuous times?

PERSUADE

God's Word influences, encourages, and guides

1. How do the valuable lessons from 1 Peter 5:10 encourage you to stand strong?

   a. Restore the broken.

   b. Stablish the unstable.

   c. Strengthen the weak.

   d. Settle the soul.

2. Jesus using spit to heal the blind man seems ridiculous. (Mark 8:23)

   a. Using Proverbs 3:5 expound on how to view this nonsensical act.

3. Mark 8:24 says the blind man looked up. Hebrews 12:2 tells us to fix our eyes on Jesus. Read Psalm 121. Respond to the following:

   a. What is our encouragement? (vs. 1)

   b. What benefit is there to looking up? (vs. 2-8)

PRACTICAL

applying Biblical Truth to present day

1. How do the following verses help you stand strong?

    a. Deuteronomy 32:4

    b. Psalm 25:4

    c. Psalm 25:10

    d. Hosea 14:9

2. Write out the beginning of the prayer found in Habakkuk 3:2.

a. What miracles of Jesus have you recently heard about or witnessed?

b. To help you stand strong, what part of Habakkuk's prayer can you pray?

PERSONAL

inviting Jesus into your current reality

1. Ellen wrote *we're easily led astray by what we think is true*. If we're not attentive, tenuousness can have us relying on emotion and illusion.

    a. When weak, how have you been led astray?

    b. What needs to change for you to stand strong?

2. Read Isaiah 42:16. When stumbling and unsure of your footing, how can this verse help your walk with Jesus?

7

strength for the HESITANT

"This is what the Lord says: 'Let not the wise man boast of his wisdom or the strong man boast of his strength or the rich man boast of his riches "
Jeremiah 9:23

I'd like to formally apologize to all English, literature, and Language Arts teachers who had me as a student. I was inattentive, lazy, and disinterested. And I'm sorry. Somehow the seeds of your labor still took root as I now love wordsmithing, reading, studying, and writing. Phraseology and syntax and expression grab my attention. Writing has become a passion. Words have become more than combinations of letters.

In preparation for this chapter, I researched (which used to be something to dread) the phrase *He who hesitates is lost*. According to sources, this expression is an adaptation of a line from the play, *Cato*, written in 1712. The original line is *The woman that deliberates is lost*.

This man-made proverb, whether in its original state or modern bent, has the same meaning – if we're undecided, uncertain, or unwilling to act in a definite way, then significant or life-changing opportunities are lost. They're inaccessible. Swift action and quick decision-making lead to success and victory.

As a young adult, I was a part of the church softball team – not for my athletic ability but to affirm and enthusiastically cheer on the team. Hesitating at the plate was commonplace for me. Hesitating as a flyball came my way may have impacted the final score a time or two. But I never hesitated to applaud or congratulate a teammate who had a nice swing, made a great catch, or handled the ball with excellence.

Interestingly, though I'm not athletic, I am competitive and driven to succeed and experience victory. The summer after cancer treatments, my family was at our usual end-of-July destination, Family Camp at Bay Shore Camp and Family Ministries (referred to as BSC) in Sebewaing, MI. Going through surgery, chemotherapy, and radiation somehow settled a deeper desire to be victorious. So, when the BSC Amazing Race was announced that year, the competitor in me came out.

The competition consisted of four-person teams contending to complete various activities. Swift action and quick decision making were necessary to compete. Our team consisted of Kevin and another couple, Rob and Jen. Using masking tape, we attached our first initial to the back of our t-shirts. We introduced our team by arranging ourselves to form Team JERK. There's no implication, only amusement.

One of the events required we harness up for the zip-line, and after we jumped, we attempted to drop tennis balls in a garbage can. I assumed only two team members needed to participate, and not liking the idea of the zip-line, I figured I'd gladly sacrifice this event to my teammates. As we were running to the zip-line, Kevin was reading the directions: *each team member must harness up.* Sacrifice quickly turned to participation.

Prior to this game, I had zero desire to zip-line. But knowing my team was counting on each of us being all-in, hesitation wasn't an option —until I was next in line to jump off the high platform. In a matter of a minute, I had a silent motivating, affirming, encouraging conversation with myself. If I wanted to succeed and be victorious, I couldn't hesitate when the zip-line boss gave us the go-ahead. She raised her hand, and as she quickly brought her arm down giving us the approval to jump, I jumped. Hesitation could not a part of the jump. Though I got zero tennis balls in the can, the success and victory came from the jump. Had I hesitated, I would have turned around and walked away, never experiencing this personal victory. After all, those who hesitate lose.

In Mark 10:17-31 we find three occasions of hesitation. Throughout this chapter, each case will be separated by sections.

Part I – Hesitant to Obey
Mark 10:17-22

KEY POINT: CURIOSITY MUST HAVE PURE MOTIVE

I'm a big-picture-but-don't-miss-any-details kind of person. Connecting the dots is important to me. Having detailed information allows the pieces of a story or a situation fit together. Asking questions, being inquisitive, and relying on intuition help to navigate my curiosity.

With intentionality we'll begin at the end of the first occurrence of hesitation. Look at Mark 10:22. It says, "At this the man's face fell. He went away sad…" Based on accounts from three Gospel writers, Matthew, Mark, and Luke, we're given three vital pieces of information.

- This man is rich.
- This man is young.
- This man is a ruler.

Based on these facts, we can surmise and speculate. Being challenged by a life-altering opportunity wouldn't intimidate this man. Situations would have warranted swift action on his part. Making quick, last-minute decisions wouldn't be stressful to this man. And, hesitation would not have served him well as a rich, young ruler.

Yet, we read he went away sad. Something grievous changed his demeanor. He suddenly went from elation to sorrow. If we only speculate, we'll miss purposeful insights, spiritual application, and opportunity to learn valuable life lessons.

According to many polls, Oreos are the world's most popular cookie. Two outer pieces house what's in the middle. Sandwiches and burgers are similarly structured – without the two outer pieces, the middle wouldn't be held together.

Mark 10:17 is one outer piece. Mark 10:22 is the other. The outer verses bring the middle ones together. Now that we have the tail end of the story, we need its beginning.

"As Jesus started on his way, a man ran up to him and fell on his knees before him. 'Good teacher,' he asked, 'what must I do to inherit eternal life?" (Mark 10:17) The same man, whose face was downcast and walked away filled with sorrow, moments earlier had approached Jesus with excitement. This verse is filled with purposeful pieces, each involving Jesus.

- A man recognizes Jesus
- A man runs to Jesus
- A man kneels before Jesus
- A man desires to be taught by Jesus
- A man asks a life-changing question of Jesus

The man, in verse twenty-two, is introduced as *a* man in verse seventeen. There was no hesitation in his approach, greeting, or reverence toward Jesus. He eagerly went all the way to the feet of Jesus and earnestly honored Him through action and word. This man didn't hesitate to speak his mind. He was not about to let this opportunity slip by. After all, those who hesitate lose.

Further reading will show us Jesus isn't alone, so in his haste he didn't bother to excuse himself or take Jesus aside for the sake of privacy. As a ruler, he understood honor and respect. As a young man, he was respectful of his elders and authorities. We can assume as a rich, young ruler, he didn't make it a habit to run up to those he desired to meet with, fall at their feet, and kneel before them. But he was compelled to approach Jesus in this manner. Perhaps he had heard about others who came to Jesus and followed their example. At first, he referred to Jesus as a *good* teacher. The adjective is telling.

In Luke 10:25 an expert of the law stood up to test Jesus and asked the same question. "What must I do to inherit eternal life?" There was no kneeling in reverence and no sincerity in his asking. His motive was to test, not be taught.

The rich, young ruler expected to be taught by the Good Teacher and was eager to learn what Jesus had to say in response to his genuine question, "What must I do to inherit eternal life?" Most voices raise at the end of a sentence when a question is being asked out loud. Of course, we're missing the inflection of his spoken words, but I imagine the emphasis fell on the two words *I do*.

Like a great deal of people, he believed actions were paramount to eternal destiny. *There must be something I can do. I need to make sure I've checked all the to-do boxes to secure my eternal home. What have I missed? Please tell me what I must do.* The rich, young ruler is more than curious; he's adamant to know the answer. His motive isn't in question, his mindset is.

KEY POINT: WHEN QUESTIONING JESUS, OUR MINDSET GETS CHALLENGED

Jesus never wasted one word, and He never misspoke. He answers the rich, young ruler with a question of His own. "Why do you call me good? No one is good – except God alone." (Mark 10:18) This is not a rebuke from Jesus. And it's not a denial of being the Good Teacher. Every word out of the mouth of Jesus was authorized and approved by God, the Father and delivered through the Holy Spirit.

It's possible the question from Jesus was to challenge the young man to consider to whom he was speaking. Yes, he was aware Jesus was a good teacher, but did he know he was face to face with the Son of God? Jesus posed a question to challenge and change this rich, young ruler's mindset.

Jesus didn't hesitate as He went on to complete the answer to the young man's question. "You know the commandments: Do not murder, do not commit adultery, do not steal, do not give false testimony, do not defraud, honor your father and mother." (Mark 10:19)

Once again, without hesitation, this man responds, "Teacher," he declared, "all these I have kept since I was a boy." (Mark 10:20)

Dear Mr. Rich, Young Ruler, your response sounds almost childlike. Que the gold star and the you-did-it sticker affixed next to the red-inked smiley face on your homework paper. This is not about a checklist. It's about obedience. Jesus quoted six of the Ten Commandments involving your attitude and behavior toward your fellow man. And He began with "You know the commandments."

It's possible Jesus was testing you to see if you'd respond by quoting or mentioning the four He didn't speak about.

- Have no other gods before God
- Do not make idols or bow to them
- Do not misuse God's name
- Remember and keep the Sabbath holy

Perhaps Jesus wanted the rich, young ruler to notice that the unmentioned commands deal with our relationship to God. Some like to say the first four are vertical, pointing and having to do with God, while the remaining six are horizontal and relate to human relationships. This man intentionally lived well toward his fellow man. He's now challenged with his vertical relationship.

When our minds are set in the wrong direction, we're weary, weak, and worn out. And we need a face-to-face encounter with Jesus. I'm not so sure this man thinks he's weary, weak, or worn out. Spiritual weariness and weakness are often masked. Satan likes it that way. His distraction and disruption are more effective to out spiritual devastation.

This man is within reach of Jesus, but before he can be face to face, Jesus has one more thing to say – and it's a life-changing challenge. How he responds has eternal implications. All too often, followers think and act based on their mindset rather than having their minds set on God's words and His ways.

- *Those who live in accordance with the Spirit have their minds set on what the spirit desires* [Romans 8:5]

- *Set your minds on things above, not on earthly things* [Colossians 3:2]
- *Be transformed by the renewing of your mind* [Romans 12:2]

God does not leave His followers in the dark. Every answer to every problem we face is found in His Word. In Jeremiah 31:33 He says, "I will put my law in their minds and write it on their hearts." The rich, young ruler could claim this promise. You and I can, too. The question is...are we willing to have our mindset reset?

KEY POINT: JUST *ONE THING* CAN KEEP US FROM THE REAL THING

Jesus roots for all of us. He cheers us on, He fights for us, and He encourages us to an abiding, close, abundant, vibrant, steady, eternal relationship with the Father. He knows things get in the way of living upright. He understands we get distracted. He sees the disruptions that take our eyes off Him.

Since the rich, young ruler was a boy, he treated others with high regard and respect, he honored his parents, he didn't break the law of his land, he was true to his wife, he didn't steal, murder, covet, or lie against his fellow man. As I consider this man, lyrics to an old hymn internally ring.

*When we walk with the Lord in the light of His Word,
what a glory He sheds on our way!
While we do His good will, He abides with us still,
and with all who will trust and obey.
Trust and obey,
for there's no other way to be happy in Jesus,*

but to trust and obey.

But we never can prove the delights of His love,
until all on the altar we lay;
for the favor He shows, for the joy He bestows,
are for all who will trust and obey.
Trust and obey,
for there's no other way to be happy in Jesus,
but to trust and obey.

The repetitive theme runs on a loop in my mind. Trust and obey. The little three-letter word in the center stands tall. It doesn't say *or*; it isn't *consider*; it's not *if you*. It doesn't suggest multiple choice. Trust *AND* obey. There is absolutely no other way to know true contentment.

According to Mark 10:21 "Jesus looked at him and loved him..." Jesus is in a conversation with this young man, but they're not yet face to face. The eyes of Jesus are on the man, but the man's eyes are on himself. *Jesus looked at him* means He turned His eye to him and considered him. And He looked out of love. Jesus loves you so much He can't take His eyes off you. With His eyes locked on the man, Jesus rocks his world with what He says.

"One thing you lack..." According to his own standards, this young man has it all and has it all together. Every box on his personal how-to-gain-eternal-life list is checked off. The real thing, eternal life, is certainly in his reach. What more can there be?

One thing.

To inherit eternal life, he lacks one thing. Out of His immeasurable love, Jesus looks into this man's soul and answers the question, challenging his mindset.

"Go, sell everything you have and give to the poor and

you will have treasure in heaven. Then come, follow me."
(Mark 10:21) In short, trust and obey. The man asked.
Jesus answered.

The sequence is clear, he must trust and obey. For
there's no other way.

Go.
Sell.
Give.
Have.
Come.
Follow.

Without hesitation, the man's face fell, and he went
away sad.

"...because he had great wealth." This rich, young
ruler was not willing to trust and obey his *one thing* to
Jesus. Therefore, it's more accurate to say his great wealth
had him rather than he had great wealth.

**KEY POINT: HESITATION IN OBEDIENCE RESULTS IN
DEVASTATION**

This man walked away from a face-to-face encounter
with Jesus because he was hesitant to obey. And it had
eternal consequences. The fact he eagerly and
enthusiastically approached Jesus shows he trusted the
good teacher. But a hesitation to obey has a devastating
outcome.

We cannot simultaneously trust earthly things and
trust Jesus. We were not created to have divided hearts.
Remember the expert in the law from Luke 10:25 who
stood and tested Jesus with his question of *What must I do
to inherit eternal life*? Since the man was an expert, Jesus

responded by challenging, "What is written in the Law? How do you read it?"

The expert combined two thoughts from the Law. "Love the Lord your God with all your heart and with all your soul and with all your strength and with all your mind; and love your neighbor as yourself." (Deuteronomy 6:5 and Leviticus 19:18)

Another three-letter word stands out in these combined Old Testament verses quoted by the expert in Luke 10:27.

All.

All cannot be divided or shared. Followers of Jesus must be careful we're not only experts in what our Good Teacher instructs, yet unwilling or hesitant to obey His instructions. A mind not fully made up, hesitates to obey and lives undecided.

If we wait for better timing to get our life in order before we fully trust and obey, we hesitate and don't stand strong. Jesus is the only one who's able to change our minds, set us straight, and meet our need. It's time we stop hesitating and trust and obey Jesus.

Jesus says, "Do this..."

- Love the Lord your God
- ...with ALL your heart
- ...with ALL your soul
- ...with ALL your strength
- ...with ALL your mind

"...and you will LIVE" (Luke 10:28)

Part II – Hesitant to Commit
Mark 10:23-27

KEY POINT: REMAIN NEAR JESUS AND BE AMAZED

The Good Teacher isn't done teaching. Instead of following the rich, young ruler who's grieving and, sadly, has walked away from Jesus, He turns His attention to the disciples who remain standing around Him. They witnessed the interaction between their Master and the rich man. Any of them could have thrown up their hands, gave in to doubt, and left with the rich young ruler.

But they remained. Followers who trust and obey, stay the course – no matter what. Even when Jesus doesn't make sense? Yes, especially then. When Jesus asked the young man about his one thing, do you think the disciples considered theirs?

Jesus looks around, makes eye contact with His disciples, and responds to the young man's departure. "How hard it is for the rich to enter the kingdom of God!"

It is what it is. If ever there was a statement that annoys me, this one is it. It's overused, vague, offensive, and leaves no room for change. Followers of Jesus have no business proclaiming this declaration to seemingly impossible situations.

I must admit, until recently I read this response from Jesus as a question. After all, it begins with a how. Furthermore, I switched the *it* and the *is*, making it *how hard is it*. To switch God's words twists the intent of His Word. In this instance, it truly is what it is – just as Jesus says – it's hard for the rich to enter the kingdom of God!

Committed to his wealth, the rich man approached Jesus. And when Jesus challenged his *one thing*, the rich man hesitated to obey, choosing wealth over eternal life. He walked away wealthy, but a sorrowful rich man is a lost man. After all, he who hesitates loses. It is hard for the rich to enter the kingdom of God.

The words of Jesus amazed His disciples. The original meaning to the Greek word for amazed is astonished and terrified. Tucking in tight to Jesus, trusting and obeying His Word, should have an effect on us. God's word is alive! It's sharp, diving to the depths of souls, challenging and changing lives. Be amazed – His word corrects, teaches, and trains. Be terrified – His Word rebukes. God does not want us afraid of Him, but we should fear what happens if we live disobedient and contrary to His ways.

Just this week, a terrible storm hit the west side of Michigan. To be exact, it was a quasi-linear convective system. Uh-huh, that. Damaging straight-line winds and torrential rain hit just as the sun was setting. I live on the east side of the state, but earlier this week I came to our home-away-from-home to write.

I'm not one to worry or become anxious. You could say I'm prewired this way. I've also not struggled (except bees and storms) with fear. If I had to choose which fear runs deeper, hands down, it's bees. Just ask my friend Amy. She decided to be a good neighbor and came to my door to introduce herself. I heard the knock, opened the door, and was greeted by an exuberant, "Hi! My name is Amy, and we just moved..." BAM! Without hesitation, I slammed the door in her face.

What else could I have done? There was a bee flying near my door! I had small children, and I was protecting them. Had the bee entered my home, I would have had to pack up the kids and run for cover. Kevin wasn't home; therefore, no one was available to kill the buzzing, stinging, fear-inducing critter.

Each of these irrational thoughts came at the speed of light, with no thought of Amy standing on the other side of the slammed door. I didn't hesitate to slam the door, but I hesitated to reopen it. I was more committed to my fear than a potential friendship. "Umm, so, yeah, uh, there was a bee...and I hate bees...and it was flying...and I didn't know...so, umm...I slammed the door in your face, and I'm so sorry." Thank God for Amy's sense of humor. She's still a dear friend who reminds me often how our friendship began.

When the winds picked up and the rain poured down, I was alone. My friend who lives nearby called and said I could come over, but I declined her offer. Don't get me wrong. I wanted to run to her house and hope our conversation and laughter would drown out the noise from the storm and settle my worried thoughts.

But God had a different plan – remain home alone and commit my fear to Him. As the storm roared, I trusted God to bring a peace that passes all understanding. (Philippians 4:7) My heart and my mind needed guarding. I looked for ways to be amazed at what God would do in my fear. In Isaiah 26:3 we have this promise: "You will keep in perfect peace him whose mind is steadfast, because he trusts in You." God desired I place my trust in Him, and it required I step away from my fear. After all, I can't stand strong when I'm face to face with fear.

The morning after the storm, I was having my personal time with Jesus – separate from the time I spend studying His Word when writing or preparing to speak and teach. Because it was the 29th of the month, I was reading Psalm 29. 3 "The voice of the Lord is over the waters; the God of glory thunders, the Lord thunders over the mighty waters. 4 The voice of the Lord is powerful; the voice of the Lord is majestic. 7The voice of the Lord strikes with flashes of lightening. 11 The Lord gives strength to his people..."

I stand amazed. When we're weary, weak, and worn out, a face-to-face encounter with Jesus strengthens us. I choose to remain firmly rooted in the presence of Jesus, standing strong through my fears, amazed at His tender-loving care.

KEY POINT: REPETITION KEEPS US FROM HESITATION

As the disciples stood amazed, Jesus repeats His words, "Children, how hard it is to enter the kingdom of God!" Then He continues with hyperbole. "It is easier for a camel to go through the eye of a needle than for a rich man to enter the kingdom of God." As a lover of word pictures, this thought makes me chuckle. Jesus uses the largest animal known in that day with the smallest opening familiar to His audience.

Their reaction? Mark 10:26 says, "The disciples were even more amazed..." But they're not terrified. Though the New International Version uses the word amazed twice, the original language uses different words. Repetitive amazement kept them focused on Jesus. But are they fully committed to understanding?

Mark 10:26 goes on "...they said to each other, 'Who then can be saved?" Doubt and uncertainty threaten their amazement. But before we tsk-tsk at the disciples, let's recognize they didn't hesitate to speak out loud. As an omniscient God, He's aware of every thought surrounding Jesus in this moment. But it's the blatant question Jesus responds to.

Still intently engaged with the disciples, Jesus has words that will encourage and inspire them and cement their faith. "With man this is impossible, but not with God; all things are possible with God." (Mark 10:27) All the wealth in the world can't save, comfort, or offer lasting joy. But Jesus can.

Mary, the mother of Jesus, heard these same words in answer to her how-can-this-be question after the angel told her she had found favor with God and as a virgin would conceive and give birth to God's Son. Luke 1:37 records the answer to her question. "For nothing is impossible with God." Doubt and uncertainty naturally came to Mary with such mind-boggling news, but her soul only gets settled if she claims God's words and trusts them. Her immediate response obliterates the uncertainty, and she commits to God's plan. "I am the Lord's servant. May it be to me as you have said." Trust and obey, for there's no other way.

Doubt and uncertainty are close by the disciples, but they haven't embraced them either. They are surely strengthened by His words, committed even deeper to their Master.

Part III – Hesitant to Surrender
Mark 10:28-30

KEY POINT: EVERYTHING CAN'T BE MISSING ANYTHING

God is an all-in God. He fully, completely, faithfully, and steadfastly loves us. Jesus came to give us life, life to the full. He fills emptiness to overflowing. In John 4, Jesus tells a woman at a well about living water, and if she were to drink of it, she'd never be thirsty – His living water would be a constant, life-giving stream, satisfying her completely.

Jesus was fully committed and completely obedient to God's plan of forgiveness. When Jesus hung on the cross, He was all in. Every sin was nailed to His cross and each repented sin is covered by His blood in a constant, never-ending flow of forgiveness.

With Jesus as our Teacher, we should follow His lead. He walked earth, fully committed to God and completely surrendered to His Father's will.

In Mark 10:28 Jesus still has the attention of His disciples. After He declared all things are possible with God, Peter spoke without hesitation. "We have left everything to follow you!" And they had. Jesus tells them the truth – nothing else will do, and nothing else could come out of Him but truth. In the King James Version, Mark 10:29 reads "And Jesus answered and said, 'Verily I say unto you...'"

When Jesus uses the word *verily* I think He's saying, "Hear ye!" But the Greek word is *amen*. That's right! What we say at the end of a prayer, Jesus says in the beginning of a thought, translating as surely or truly. When used at the end of a discourse, it means so be it or so it is. And here we find an acceptable use for *it is what it is*.

Amen is said to be the best-known word in human speech. It's found in a vast array of languages with the meaning never changing. Here in Mark 10:29-30, Jesus uses it to strengthen His disciples as He affirms their decision to leave everything and follow Him.

Leaving everything is confusing at times. We think of leaving as stepping away, moving out, giving up, and never returning. There are times when God requires His children to leave a career, give up a bank account, sell a house, or step away from a community. But full surrender is more about our willingness to step away, move away, or give away.

When we're hesitant to surrender an unhealthy habit, a character flaw, a bad attitude, jealousy, rudeness, worry, envy, disrespect, immoral behavior, lust, lying, pride, gluttony – anything that stands in the way of a full-on, face-to-face encounter with Jesus, we need to remember He gave His everything, that we might live.

Followers of Jesus will never miss anything God has

for them if they don't hesitate to obey, commit, and surrender to Him.

PONDER

deeply, carefully, and thoughtfully consider

1. Describe how your walk with Jesus gets affected when you are:

    a. Hesitant to obey

    b. Hesitant to commit

    c. Hesitant to surrender

2. Consider how much God loves you. How do you know He loves you?

a. Do you stand amazed at His provision?

b. Do you stand amazed at His protection?

c. Explain.

PERSUADE

God's Word influences, encourages, and guides

1. Read Proverbs 24:10. Faltering is a form of hesitation. What do you learn about your strength from this verse?

2. Waiting can have us hesitant to believe in God's presence through our struggles. God's Word teaches how to stand strong when in the waiting times of life. How do the following verses help you to stand strong and avoid hesitancy as you wait?

    a. Titus 2:11-13

    b. Isaiah 30:18

c. Psalm 130

d. Psalm 40:1-3

PRACTICAL

applying Biblical Truth to present day

1. In Mark 10:21 Jesus looked at the rich, young ruler, He loved the rich, young ruler, and He spoke to the rich, young ruler. He told the man he lacked *one thing*.

a. What *one thing* keeps you from full surrender?

b. Notice the progression of verbs from this verse. Don't think literal, but how can you apply these words to stand strong in your walk with Jesus?

- Go

- Sell

- Give

- Come

- Follow

c. Compare James 4:7-8 with Mark 10:22.

a. The rich, young ruler went away sad. Perhaps pride was in the way.

According to James 4:7 what four things combat pride.

_____ yourselves

_____ the devil

_____ near to God

_____ your hands, _____ your heart

d. Read Mark 10:27. Do you wholeheartedly believe this? Explain.

PERSONAL

inviting Jesus into your current reality

1. What causes you to hesitate to obey God's commands?

2. How does the rich, young ruler's story compare to your life?

3. We stand strong when our mind is set on God's will, His Word, and His ways. What area in your life is God challenging you to allow Him to change your mindset?

8
strength for the UNDERVALUED

"¹¹ One thing God has spoken, two things I have heard:
that you, O God, are strong,
¹² and that you, O lord, are loving.
Surely you will reward each person according
to what he has done."
Psalm 62:11-12

Undervalued is not an adjective commonly used. Many feel it...few admit it. Recently, I posted a picture of a straight and long wooden-planked bridge to my personal Facebook page. In the picture, near the bottom, stood the word undervalued. Posting the picture, I wrote, "Comment, please. What comes to mind as you consider this word?" Over fifty comments were made. I've rooted out the short and applicable responses.

Unworthy. Depression. Left out. Unloved. Unappreciated. Victim. Me. Invisible and unnoticed. Anger. Sadness. People. Unimportant. Taken for granted. Unheard. Misunderstood. Striving hard to prove/Giving up in despair. Shame.

Because I'm familiar with most of my 'friends' on social media, the responses I mentioned here are from people who claim to walk with Jesus. Feeling unworthy causes weariness. Feeling undervalued brings about weakness. Seeking worth, significance, and value in anything other than Jesus will have us worn-out.

KEY POINT: BE INCLINED TO RECLINE AND DINE

A hectic lifestyle is a common and accepted lifestyle. It's the reason we don't rest well. Unrested folks are weary, weak, and worn out. Mark 14:3 says Jesus was reclining at Simon the Leper's table. Reclining, lying on one's side, or propped up by the elbow was common back then. A good meal, invited guests, and slow eating indicate reclining to be a welcomed custom.

In today's culture, it seems reclining is mostly welcomed after a Thanksgiving feast or reserved for Sunday afternoons. During the week, we're more inclined to dine in our SUV's or on the sofa, with our invited guests on the television or computer screen.

In our family, with our youngest two still at home, Kevin and I desire the evening meal be a priority. However, being in ministry, involved at our church and engaged in community events, managing athletic practices and contests, music lessons, and extra-curricular activity, we understand a missed meal will occur. Our four adult kids are married and live hours apart; expecting everyone to be present on a regular basis is unreasonable. Instead of complaining or mourning the meals we miss, we're inclined to be grateful for the times we do gather.

For thirty years, when eating our evening meal together, we recline at our dinner table. I use reclining in the spirit of the word, as our current dining option is a high-top table. For us Harbin's, reclining involves conversing, taking our time to eat, and remaining at the table long after the food is eaten because we like to recline and dine together.

- Dine: to entertain at dinner
- Recline: lean, lie back, rest in an inactive position

You can be assured, Harbin's know how to dine. Need

entertainment? Come to the Harbin house, recline at our table – you'll experience many facets of what we deem entertainment to be. When the whole Harbin family is together, we squeeze around the table. Even in our small-ish dining space, we still recline, and we dine.

It's our goal no one leave this space undervalued. Over the years, Kevin and I have heard our kids voice their dreams, sorrows, goals, struggles, breakups, and inspirations while at the table. Graduations, weddings, adoption, moving, and career changes are talked about. We've celebrated the highs and we've cried over lows. As we dine, we pray. As we recline, we discuss and debate, banter and brawl, and offer approval and apology.

When our four older kids were teens, most of their friends had cell phones. We were late to that party. Our dining table became, and still is, a cell-free zone. We can't effectively recline and dine while distracted.

I believe we have a responsibility to intentionally recline and dine together as much as possible with the people we deeply love and care about. It plays a part in effecting confidence, connectedness, belonging, acceptance, communication, and worth. If Jesus reclined and dined, shouldn't we?

KEY POINT: JESUS CHANGES WHAT YOU WERE, NOW BE OK WITH WHO YOU ARE

In Mark 14:3 we read where Jesus is reclining at the home of Simon the Leper. If anyone should feel undervalued, it's Simon. Why can't Mark just say Jesus was reclining at Simon's house? Why the qualifier? Why the identity marker? Why tell us what he used to be?

This thinking will have us weary, weak, and worn out in no time. We struggle to be reminded of who we were before Jesus saved us. Mark isn't throwing *leper* in Simon's face – he's showing us what happens when Jesus is invited in and welcomed at the table.

Lepers were societal outcasts. They were shunned, ignored, and avoided. Lepers lived with other lepers in colonies on the outskirts of town. When they came to market or had reason to be in the public realm, they had to cry out, "Unclean, unclean!" to warn people they were passing by.

Scripture doesn't say, but Simon must have been healed by Jesus. The only way he could dwell at home would be if he was no longer leprous. Then why call him Simon, the leper, if Jesus healed him? If we live every day in a face-to-face encounter with Jesus, if our relationship with Him is current and up to date, and if we've been set free from our past, then we won't struggle if the whole world were to know what we used to be.

Simon the Leper has been healed. And Jesus is reclining and dining at his house. I wonder how many of our neighbors or coworkers or folks in the Starbuck's drive-thru or moms in the pick-up line at the elementary school would turn to Jesus if we posted yard signs, placed bumper stickers, hung posters, rented billboards, or flew banners declaring what we used to be?

The interpretation of the posted declarations can only be accurately explained by how we live our everyday life. If we live bothered, broken, baffled, or belligerent because we feel undervalued, then how can those around us see Jesus through us?

Rahab's story (see Joshua Chapter two) occurs hundreds of years before the writer of Hebrews mentions her by name. Hebrews 11:31 says, "By faith, the prostitute Rahab..." She gave up her old life and lived a life pleasing to God. He was her Rock, her Refuge, and her Redeemer.

In Matthew Chapter one, there are only five women named in the genealogy of Jesus, and Rahab is one. Rahab, *the prostitute*, is named in the lineage of God's Son, the Savior of the world! Rahab's value doesn't come in what she isn't any longer; it comes through the saving grace of her Redeemer.

Simon the Leper's value doesn't come from what he used to be; it comes from the one who healed him and made him whole. Being reminded of what we used to be isn't to make us weary, weak, and worn out. It's to show the world around us who Jesus is and how He can change a person surrendered to Him.

KEY POINT: WHEN WE SURRENDER ALL, WE NEVER CEASE SURRENDERING

"...a woman came..." (Mark 14:3) We know from John 12:3, this woman is Mary, the sister of Martha and Lazarus. She's come face-to-face with Jesus before. Her actions at Simon the Leper's house prove she lives face to face with Jesus every day. But before we look at what she did, let's get to know her better.

We're introduced to Mary in Luke 10:38-41 after Martha, her sister, opened their home to Jesus. Mary's encounter with Jesus that day teaches us how to live a life of surrender.

- She sat at His feet
- She listened to what he said

Mary literally sat at the feet of Jesus, but we can live as if we've claimed the same posture. When I was in the early grades of elementary school, I was often in trouble for talking too much. Report cards from kindergarten state

"Ellen distracts the other children during rest time." Ok, I'm not in defensive mode, but rest time? In kindergarten? How does that help an extroverted child?

In first grade, as my sister Susan and I walked in the door from school, mom would greet us with the expected "Hi, girls, how was your day?" I'm not sure if she was hoping for a different response, but I always replied, "Great!" followed by Susan's, "I saw Ellen's desk in the hall again." Second grade was no different.

Still today, without any awareness and when mingling with others as a circle of people forms, I find myself in the center. It's very subtle, but when I realize it, I step back and join the perimeter. I remember in kindergarten, when the teacher would call us students to gather around her feet for reading time, I'd run to the center of the rug – it's where the out-going and socializing ones were most comfortable. And every time the teacher would say, "Ellen, why don't you come and sit right near me." Her *why* statement never ended with a question mark.

She was a wise teacher. Sitting at her feet offered less distraction and allowed her to have and keep my attention. If my focus altered, a simple touch on my head or shoulder would bring me back. Being at the feet of Jesus has less distractions – it's where we listen best.

Mary listened to what Jesus said. Parents are constantly inquiring, "Did you hear me?" to their children. Oh, Mary heard Jesus, but she also listened, she understood, she perceived, and she comprehended. Sitting at His feet positions us to hear what He says so we can live what He teaches.

In John Chapter eleven we read the story of Jesus raising Mary's brother, Lazarus, from the dead. In John 11:29-33 Mary heard Jesus had arrived at their village, and she quickly got up and ran to meet Him. When she reached the place where Jesus was, she fell at His feet. Surrendered followers know where to find their strength – daily dwelling at the feet of Jesus.

Mark 14:3 says Mary didn't come empty handed. There is always something we can bring to Jesus. Today, on-line giving is convenient to the giver and an act of wise stewardship from a ministry perspective. When I was a child, weekly envelopes were provided for people to bring their tithes and offerings to church and place in the offering plate. They were created as a means of convenience and assistance for giving. Even the children had envelopes. I remember my parents saying, "Don't forget your offering envelope." I can almost recall the taste of the seal as I would enclose my gift to God. I was confident my dime would help the cause of Christ.

It's not about the church getting the gift; it's more about the giver needing to give. Financially giving to God is only one way we're taught to give. We should give our talents and our time, as well. But not out of obligation. We come to Jesus out of love and gratefulness and obedience. A surrendered heart is a surrendered life. 'In the Bleak Midwinter' is one of my favorite Christmas hymns.

What can I give him, poor as I am?
If I were a shepherd, I would give a lamb;
If I were a Wise Man, I would do my part;
Yet what I can give him;
Give my heart.

Mary lived surrendered to Jesus and was attuned to His teaching. As Mary approached Jesus, she was aware the chief priests and teachers of the law were looking to arrest Him. Her brother was at the table dining with Jesus, Martha was serving the reclining men, and Mary was present with her gift.

KEY POINT: WORLDLY VALUE IS OVER-RATED

Mark 14:3 continues, Mary brought to Jesus "...an alabaster jar of very expensive perfume, made of pure nard..." This jar was more like a flask made of the same stone used for caskets. Interestingly, Good Friday is only a few days away. Mary brought her gift out of her devotion to Jesus, not preparation for His death.

The King James Version says Mary came with *an alabaster box of ointment of spikenard very precious.* In that day, the most precious and valuable ointments were prepared with the pleasant-smelling juice from the nard, the spike or head of a fragrant plant native to a far-off land.

Mark says the contents of this alabaster jar was very expensive. The costly perfume was extremely precious and should be reserved for a special moment. Her use of this valuable perfume would not meet societal expectations at a casual gathering. But Mary didn't bring the box because of the value of the contents. The contents were valuable because the recipient was worthy of them.

We are inundated with what the world around us says is valuable. Two purses next to each other on a rack at any department store can significantly vary in price. The same shape, color, material, pattern, and inside compartments make them appear to be identical. But the name changes the value.

It's no different with cars, clothes, furniture, and zip codes – the name alters the value. Some people get caught in the web of worldly value. Whatever the item, if culture determines its worth, then it's worthy of ownership. Followers of Jesus must be careful with this mindset. Having costly things is not the problem. When the costly things own us, that's an obstacle causing missteps on our faith journey.

KEY POINT: BROKEN AND POURED OUT

Mark 14:3 continues, "...She broke the jar and poured the perfume on his head..." Matthew agrees. John, however, reports she poured it on Jesus' feet and, then wiped them with her hair. Though anointing was customary at feasts, she broke custom because it was a matter of the heart. The discrepancy of head or feet is not our emphasis.

Her desire to be broken at His feet, and her passion to pour it on Him is the focal point. A woman who brings her broken pieces to Jesus is strengthened by Him. A woman who pours her passions, her dreams, her expectations, and longings on Jesus stands strong.

A broken woman shouldn't be concerned with her value because Jesus states her worth, and she's valued by Him. Followers who struggle with feeling undervalued need self-examination. My friend Sharon says, "You will feel yourself to be undervalued every time you allow your value to be determined by someone else's reaction to some good you have done."

Too many women care too much about what others have to say or think about them. When we live for Jesus, His opinion matters most. Yes, the things people say can hurt, but before you let them determine your value, examine the truth of their words.

The word *poured* Mark uses means to pour down or pour over. Mary didn't trickle the contents of her broken box. A farmer cannot reap a valuable harvest from a sprinkle of rain. A beautiful flower garden will flourish from a good downpour. We get weary, weak, and worn out when we hold on to brokenness and don't pour it on Jesus.

Mary came prepared to spill the precious contents on Jesus. She didn't carry this alabaster box with her on the chance she'll need it. No! This plan to bring this offering formed long before she entered the house. She walked in the room confident of a face to face encounter with Jesus. The Spirit of God woos us to Jesus.

Remember Bill and Ruth? Bill was in that revival service because God invited him. Ruth went with an expectation to meet Jesus, Bill didn't have a clue, but they both came face-to-face with Him, because the Spirit of God drew them both to the feet of Jesus.

Followers of Jesus have the invaluable benefit of coming face to face with Jesus anytime, anywhere, and for any reason. God led me to create an annual women's conference. In November of 2017 the first STAND conference occurred in southeast Michigan. Before each conference, the prayer team specifically prays that women would come with an understanding of areas in their life that need to be broken and poured out to Jesus. We believe the Holy Spirit initiates and works in the hearts of women long before the conference begins.

Whether secrets from the past or current struggles, they must be broken and poured on Jesus; otherwise, we're weary, weak, and worn out. We can walk into church, participate in Bible Study, or attend conferences and retreats, but if we pretend everything is fine and refuse to break, we won't experience the invaluable healing and wholeness Jesus offers.

Why are we afraid to tell Jesus what he already knows? Why are we intimidated to surrender everything? Perhaps it has something to do with how we think others will respond to us being broken and poured out.

Falling at His feet, handing over our brokenness, pouring everything on Jesus is risky. But hoarding things meant to be surrendered is a stockpile of weariness and weakness that brings no value to our lives. Followers should act/live outside the box. Others will notice, you can be sure. They'll pay attention. God plans it that way when we're broken and poured out at the feet of Jesus.

KEY POINT: IGNORANCE PRECEEDS INDIGNATION

Mark 14:4-5 reports what some had to say about Mary's broken box with its contents on Jesus. [4] "Some of those present were saying indignantly to one another, 'Why this waste of perfume? [5] It could have been sold for more than a year's wages and the money given to the poor.' And they rebuked her harshly." Followers of Jesus need to watch their tone.

People in the Christian community are misunderstood, their words misconstrued, and their motives questioned. A few minutes on social media proves this true. The snag with social media, texting, and email is monologue. Productive debate requires conversation. And that involves speaking *and* listening.

I have a writer friend who was accused by one of her friends of plagiarism and stealing ideas. In the world of writing and speaking, those are big offenses. The accusatory turned inflammatory before my friend could respond with truth and grace. The one accusing did it through an email, discharging blame through her written accusations spewed across a screen while avoiding, shutting down really, any opportunity for dialogue.

This woman was indignant...because she was ignorant. When followers of Jesus are unaware, they're ignorant –

not stupid, rather uninformed. She didn't have all the pieces and she based her accusations on assumptions. And instead of asking questions, assumptions turned to ammunition as she hurled indictments and ended a friendship. Ignorant quickly turned unwilling, refusing to change her misguided notions.

Some of the men reclining with Jesus were ignorant, and it recklessly turned indignant.

- What they said
- How they said it

Based on their awareness, what they said isn't the bigger issue. First, they spoke under their breath. Their motive wasn't manipulative; they were just appalled at her extravagant gift and action. Secondly, they're correct. The contents of her box are worth more than a year's wage. Third, they're right. Some would choose to give their valuable possessions to the needy. It's *how* they communicated their ignorance that causes indignation.

They were indignant and rebuked her harshly. The King James Version says they murmured against her. They shared their displeasure by sternly admonishing her with a threatening tone as if they were the anointing police, determining the value of the gift, ignorant to the motive or its eternal worth. God accepts all gifts that are offered with a pure motive and useful for His kingdom. He is the one to determine the value of gifts and offerings, not onlookers, bystanders, or assumption makers.

KEY POINT: TO OBEY IS BETTER THAN SACRIFICE

In 1 Samuel 15:22 Samuel, the prophet, says, "Does the Lord delight in burnt offerings and sacrifices as much as in obeying the voice of the Lord? To obey is better than sacrifice, and to heed is better than the fat of rams."

Notice the action on our part in this passage. Obedience. Sacrifice. Heed. Look at the original meaning.

- Obey = to hear, listen to, and obey
- Sacrifice = sacrifices and offerings
- Heed = harken, be attentive, give attention, listen

Mary obediently offered her precious sacrifice and was ready and willing to hear from Jesus. As the indignant onlookers, bystanders, and assumption makers spoke meanly about her and harshly to her, she never took her eyes off Jesus. She didn't allow their voices or their words to distract or dissuade her planned offering or undervalue her sacrificial giving.

Jesus shows support of her actions by saying to them, "Leave her alone," which translates, *leave her to me*. Then He asks them a rhetorical question to correct their thinking. "Why are you bothering her?" In other words, *why beat her up with your words?*

For some of you, this is your reality. You've been verbally beaten up and emotionally brought down. It's time you open that box and pour it out on Jesus. Pour every biting, hurtful, accusing, stabbing word on Him. As you keep your eyes on Jesus, picture our Savior turning to the one who inflicted the hurt on you and witness Him say to them, "Leave her alone." *Leave her to me*.

I'm all for a strong-willed woman asserting herself and telling her tormenter or tyrant to back off, knock it off, or shout, "Enough!" Certain times call for confrontation. Ultimately, Jesus fights our battles, and when we're in a face-to-face encounter with Him, He reveals what brokenness needs to be poured on Him. So, keep your gaze fixed on Him. Our obedience to His instructions, commands, and authority is a sacrificial offering to our Savior and Lord.

KEY POINT: FULL SURRENDER IS BEAUTIFUL AND LEAVES A LEGACY

Jesus has more to say to the ignorant ones reclining and dining in His presence. A fully surrendered follower stands strong. Will we experience weariness, suffer weakness, and struggle when worn out from brokenness and feelings of unworthiness? Of course, we will. That's why a faith journey is walked out daily with Jesus. Mary's face-to-face encounter teaches us three significant lessons if we're to fully surrender our hearts – the good and the bad, the broken, and the beautiful – to Jesus.

- She has done a beautiful thing
- She did what she could
- What she has done is her legacy

She has done a beautiful thing.

John describes Mary pouring the perfume on Jesus' feet and then wiping them with her hair. Commentary tells us respectable women didn't unbind their hair in public. Remember this isn't a dinner party. This is a meal shared by those closest to Jesus. He knew His cross loomed; they only knew He was being sought to be killed. Either way, death was imminent. Before the fragrance of expensive perfume hit his nostrils, Jesus noticed the sweet fragrance of deep devotion and lasting love for Him. Perfume on His head, ointment on His feet, both were a beautiful thing because her obedience brought the sacrifice.

In a few days, Jesus would be dead. And as he stated,

the poor will still be around. The people in earshot will have plenty of opportunity to give to the needy and meet the needs of the poor. But Jesus won't always be reclining with them at the table.

She did what she could.

In Mark 14:8 Jesus says, "She did what she could. She poured perfume on my body beforehand to prepare for my burial." Jewish custom used oils on a corpse before burial, unless the dead person was a criminal, then anointing was prohibited. Commentaries say Jesus anticipated suffering a criminal's death. Prophets had proclaimed His birth (Isaiah 7:14) and His death (Isaiah 53:3 & 7). As He spoke to these men around the table, Jesus was connecting pieces of prophecy to current reality, though they couldn't wrap their minds around His impending death.

Mary would not have the literal feet of Jesus to sit at and learn from or fall at to express adoration and reverence. His death was days away, His resurrection was assured, but in less than three months from this moment, His ascension back to heaven was imminent.

So, while at His feet, she did what she could. No one can sit at His feet for us. We can't ask a friend to save us a seat. We must do what we can – get to Jesus; we must bring our brokenness, our offerings, our very lives, and stay put. My friend, Rebecca, says Mary didn't do what someone else could. Mary did what Mary could. Each follower of Jesus has a reserved place at His feet, and we are all expected to do what He calls and wills us to do.

Feeling undervalued keeps us stuck, unable to do what we can for Jesus. Getting our attention off what we feel and focus on how Jesus feels about us allows us to do what we can out of love and obedience to our Savior.

What she has done is her legacy.

Jesus continues in Mark 14:9: "I tell you the truth, wherever the gospel is preached throughout the world, what she has done will also be told, in memory of her." Every time a follower of Jesus sits at His feet and does what she can, the Gospel spreads and Mary's legacy lives on. The Gospel in invaluable to humanity. As followers of Jesus, we participate in kingdom growth when we leave this kind of legacy as we stand firm and strong in Jesus.

Returning to John 11:29-32, Mary is grieving the death of her brother Lazarus. John 11:31 says, "When the Jews who had been with Mary in the house, comforting her, noticed how quickly she got up and went out, they followed her..." One of the greatest lessons God continues to reveal to me is that there is always someone paying attention to how I face trial, tragedy, and trouble.

If we desire to leave a legacy, it's imperative and invaluable to remain at the feet of Jesus for the Gospel of Jesus to be seen in us. Mary's brother has died, and he's been buried. But when Jesus comes on the scene, she steps away from her grief and goes to Jesus. There are people paying attention to Mary's actions and attitude. Some of you want to give Mary a break and claim she's allowed to fall apart in her grief. It's going be ok if Mary turns to worldly comforts in her mourning; after all, she's human and she's hurting.

It's been weeks since my mom's death. I was talking with my dad this week, inquiring how he's doing. My dad is wise and has deep insight. Through this recent conversation he left another legacy of words. "You know Ellen, I'll have times of sadness, but I'm always reminded mom's days were ordained for her before one of them came to be. Each time I'm sad, as I miss my wife, it's a praise-the-Lord-situation. It can't be anything but."

As the grief comes, dad doesn't ignore it, but like Mary, he chooses to step away from it and be at the feet of Jesus. You can look long and hard through Scripture and you will never find where God gives permission for us to lack faith through hardship. Crisis, grief, loss, trouble, and feeling undervalued is a time to draw close to the Father. Mary stepped away from the comfort of her friends and chose to fall at the feet of Jesus.

And her friends followed her.

When we've allowed hardship to undervalue us, we've stepped off God's steady and sturdy foundation. When difficulty makes us weary, weak, and worn out, that's not the time to place our trust in people and man-made programs. People can be helpful, and programs can assist in our betterment, but none can replace the security, safety, and refuge found in the posture Mary demonstrates.

Psalm 62:11-12 gives us hope and value to our walk with Jesus. [11] "One thing God has spoken, two things I have heard: that you, O God, are strong, [12] and that you, O Lord, are loving. Surely you will reward each person according to what he has done."

God is strong. God is loving. God rewards the one who does what she could. There is no room for feeling undervalued when we stand strong at the feet of Jesus.

PONDER

deeply, carefully, and thoughtfully consider

1. What comes to your mind when you consider the word undervalued?

2. Since Jesus changed who you were, are you okay with you are? Explain.

3. How has your walk with Jesus been affected from self-worth being shaped by culture?

PERSUADE

God's Word influences, encourages, and guides

1. Where was Mary?   What was Mary doing?

John 11:32   _____   _____

Luke 10:39   _____   _____

2. What is significant about this posture?

3. How are you encouraged by Mark 14:6?

4. Read 1 Samuel 15:22.

    a. What pleases God most?

    b. What's easier to do, obey or sacrifice? Explain.

5. Read Psalm 62:11-12.

    a. What two things can we know about God?

    b. How are we rewarded?

6. Read Mark 14:8. How does this influence you to stand strong?

PRACTICAL

applying Biblical Truth to present day

1. Read Mark 14:3. What in your life needs to be broken and poured out on Jesus?

2. Read Mark 14:4-5.

   a. How has ignorance made you indignant toward another?

   b. What could you have done differently?

3. In Mark 14:9 Jesus says what Mary did will leave a legacy.

      a. What kind of spiritual legacy will you leave?

      b. Mary did what she could. What beautiful thing can you do for Jesus?

PERSONAL

inviting Jesus into your current reality

1. Ellen wrote *Seeking worth, significance, and value in anything other than Jesus will have us worn out.* Have you experienced this?

    Describe your feelings.

2. In Hebrews 11:31 Rahab is mentioned by name. She lived hundreds of years earlier, yet the writer refers to what she used to be — a prostitute. Her value doesn't come in what she was; it comes through the saving grace of her Redeemer.

a. Do you struggle with your self-worth because of what you used to be, what was done to you, or what others said about you?

b. What can you do to stand strong and not feel undervalued?

3. Mary's value came from being at the feet of Jesus. We don't have His literal feet, but what could this look like in your life today?

CONTACT

INFORMATION

Email ellen@ellenharbin.com

- If you'd like to keep updated on Ellen's speaking and writing.

- If you're interested in having Ellen speak at your women's retreat, conference, or event.

- If you'd like to have Ellen as a guest (via SKYPE, Facebook Live, or Google Hangouts) at your *STAND strong* Bible study.

- If you'd like to discuss hosting a STAND Women's Conference at your church or in your community.

ABOUT THE AUTHOR

Ellen Harbin is a gifted Bible teacher and conference speaker creatively applying the truth of God's Word to all of life's triumphs and challenges. Ellen is the founder and visionary to the STAND women's conference which is held annually in southeast Michigan. As a speaker, Ellen is engaging, inspiring, and easy to listen to, all while guiding and encouraging you to take a closer look at your relationship with Jesus and live as He intends.

Ellen and Kevin, a pastor, have been married 30 years and live in Michigan. They love to go on dates, hold hands, and spend time with family. Ellen and Kevin have six children – four biological and two through adoption. Recently, and within 17 months, three daughters-in-law and a son-in-law joined their family.

Highlights of Ellen's life include laughing hard, writing, deep conversations, spontaneity, sunrises, and spending quality time with friends – adding coffee is a bonus.

Ellen declares being a follower of Jesus is the absolute, best decision she has ever made and loves influencing others to live as He intends.

Made in the USA
Middletown, DE
13 September 2019